QUICK. EASY. HEALTHY.

GOOD FOOD EVERY DAY

CALLUM HANN & THEMIS CHRYSSIDIS

MURDOCH BOOKS

SYDNEY · LONDON

Community Learning & Libraries
Cymuned Ddysgu a Llyfrgelloedd

This item should be returned or renewed by the last date stamped below.

```
----------------------------    ----------------------------    ----------------------------

----------------------------    ----------------------------    ----------------------------

----------------------------    ----------------------------    ----------------------------

----------------------------    ----------------------------    ----------------------------

----------------------------    ----------------------------    ----------------------------

----------------------------    ----------------------------    ----------------------------

----------------------------    ----------------------------    ----------------------------

----------------------------    ----------------------------    ----------------------------

----------------------------    ----------------------------    ----------------------------
```

To renew visit:

www.newport.gov.uk/libraries

CONTENTS

INTRODUCTION

We've been working together since 2011,
although we use the term 'working' very loosely.

That's when we started Sprout Cooking School in Adelaide, South Australia—getting people into the kitchen and sharing our belief that food should be fresh, seasonal and enjoyable. Until we began Sprout, it's fair to say neither of us understood what people meant when they said, 'Find a job that you love and you'll never work a day in your life.' Well, now we do. We love our work. Talking about healthy eating, promoting real food, enjoying great meals with friends and family, and educating others about the importance of local, seasonal produce. We haven't worked a day since 2011.

'Quick, Easy & Healthy' was the very first cooking class we ever held, and it's really at the heart of our cooking philosophy. So when we were given the opportunity to turn what is now our most popular cooking class into a cookbook, we jumped at the chance.

This book is all about getting people of all ages into the kitchen and cooking delicious food that's good for you. We don't believe in health products, 'superfoods', 'diets' or strict eating plans. We just believe in food: food that doesn't cost a fortune or require expensive equipment; food that is nutritious, simple and convenient to make; and most of all food that the whole family will enjoy.

You don't need to be an amazing chef to have fun in the kitchen and create dishes that you can be proud of. You just need to have a positive attitude and desire to learn. Cooking is a skill that can be learnt over time and definitely improved upon with practice. Learning to cook helps improve our understanding of what we are putting into our body, and it inspires good food choices that you will carry with you forever. We see food as a social glue bringing people together, and the key to a healthy and happy life.

So what are we waiting for? Let's get cooking!

THE IMPORTANCE OF SEASONAL PRODUCE

Seasonality is a very important concept when creating fresh, healthy and delicious food. Seasonality refers to the weather conditions such as temperature, rainfall and sunlight which, at certain levels, facilitate optimal growth of specific fruits and vegetables. As a result of these factors, fruits and vegetables grow and ripen at different rates, depending on the time of year. When produce is growing and developing to its potential in optimal conditions, it is referred to as being 'in season'. Meat, particularly seafood, can also be considered seasonal, as certain weather conditions affect feeding patterns, breeding conditions and location or habitat.

No single fruit or vegetable (or any food for that matter!) provides us with all the nutrition we require to be healthy. This is why variety within a meal, over a day, over a week and over a year is important for good health. We need to be constantly eating a wide variety of foods to ensure we meet our nutrition requirements.

Seasonality is nature's way of ensuring we enjoy a variety of foods throughout the year, ensuring our diet is interesting and nutritionally complete. The fruits and vegetables that are in season often coincide with what our bodies need, and reflect what we like to eat and cook at that time of the year. For example, citrus fruits are in abundance in winter and are a great source of vitamin C, which can help fight off those pesky colds and bugs. Similarly, root vegetables such as potatoes and carrots flourish in winter and lend themselves well to roasts or slow-cooked meals, which is precisely the comfort food that many of us enjoy in cooler months.

By understanding the role seasonality plays in our food supply, we can establish a healthy foundation for our food choices, increasing our opportunity to consume a wider variety of foods throughout the year, and ultimately increase our intake of nutrient-rich fruits and vegetables.

Why buy seasonal produce?

COST

When produce is in season there is, naturally, more of it. Growing produce during its peak harvest time also requires less intervention. This leads to greater supply and reduced costs. If the produce is in season, it can be sourced close to home, so costs associated with freight, packaging or taxes are likely to be much lower.

FLAVOUR AND QUALITY

When produce is in season it is growing in its most optimal conditions. This will therefore impact flavour and texture. The longer something is able to grow before being harvested, the better it will taste. Produce that has been transported from overseas or interstate, has usually been harvested early to prevent it from deteriorating before sale, and to ensure it has a moderate shelf life. As a result, the flavour and texture are often inferior to the same produce freshly picked.

Some fruits and vegetables stop ripening as soon as they are picked. Others continue to ripen and develop the visual characteristics we might expect from them, however, they will more than likely lack their delicious, natural flavour if picked too early. Take, for example, tomatoes. Yes they are available all year round, but it is easy to tell the difference between a summer and winter tomato. The summer tomato is firm, sweet and bursting with flavour, while the winter tomato is often floury, soft and tasteless. The flavourless tomato will probably also cost more.

The next time you introduce anyone to a new fruit or vegetable, make sure it is in season. The best way to win over fussy eaters is for them to try foods when they are at their best!

THE NEXT TIME YOU INTRODUCE ANYONE TO A NEW FRUIT OR VEGETABLE, MAKE SURE IT IS IN SEASON. THE BEST WAY TO WIN OVER FUSSY EATERS IS FOR THEM TO TRY FOODS WHEN THEY ARE AT THEIR BEST.

NUTRITION

To maintain good health, our bodies need a variety of vitamins and minerals. Some of these are produced by the human body, but others must be obtained through our diet. Plants have the ability to synthesise some vitamins and minerals, but they also obtain a large proportion of them from the soil they are grown in. When we consume fruit and vegetables we benefit from this nutritional goodness.

When produce is grown out of season, or harvested before it has grown to its optimal ripeness, it has not had the opportunity to acquire its full complement of nutrition. In fact, studies have shown that as much as 50 per cent of vitamin potential can be lost from growing out-of-season produce.

SUSTAINABILITY AND THE ENVIRONMENT

'Sustainable foods' are foods that have little or no detrimental effect on the environment, creating no ecological carbon footprint. The production, packaging and transportation of food all results in greenhouse gas emissions and, considering most of us eat three to six times a day, the food choices we make have a major impact on the environment. Now, we aren't going so far as to suggest you have to stop eating packaged products and that we should all cycle to farmers' markets to buy groceries on the weekend, but we can think about realistic, achievable ways to reduce our carbon footprint. And purchasing seasonal foods is a great place to start.

Eating with the seasons means sourcing food that is readily available and, more often than not, grown close by. This reduces your carbon footprint by reducing emissions related to travel and packaging. Eating with the seasons also helps to reduce the need to over-harvest the land. By leaving fields fallow for some time of the year helps ensure that the nutrient content of the soil remains high.

Another way we can help to ensure we have plenty of sustainable nutritious food is to only buy what we need. Every year, households waste huge amounts of money on food that they end up throwing out. Not only is it a waste of resources, produce and money, but it also creates unnecessary landfill, which then adds to greenhouse gas emissions. Over-purchasing also drives prices up, and for some lower income households this can lead to certain basic foods becoming unattainable.

EATING WITH THE SEASONS MEANS SOURCING FOOD THAT IS READILY AVAILABLE AND, MORE OFTEN THAN NOT, WAS GROWN CLOSE BY, REDUCING YOUR CARBON FOOTPRINT.

Why has seasonality become a forgotten concept?

While most of us appreciate that certain fruits and vegetables grow well at specific times of the year, in the global, 'want-now, have-now' society we currently live in, few of us can confidently recall what is in season. When we shop at the supermarket we are spoilt for choice with an array of fresh produce from all over the world. It is astounding (and frustrating) when individuals cry out for supermarkets to support local farmers, yet these same individuals demand out-of-season produce which has to be sourced from the other side of the world. They're actually feeding the cycle they are trying to break!

As the demand for out-of-season produce increases, technology advances to facilitate the harvesting and storage of out-of-season produce to make it more readily available. This leads to a reduction in the cost of transporting foods from far away due to more efficient processes, which makes the produce increasingly affordable and continues to feed the cycle.

On top of all this, the modern world is becoming more urbanised, creating a disconnect from the origins of food. Children live in high-rise apartments without gardens, parents don't shop at all and instead have food delivered and some homes are now even built without kitchens!

The availability of out-of-season produce at supermarkets and on restaurant menus, follows a demand from consumers and their lack of understanding about seasonal produce. It's up to us to change our patterns and make local, seasonal produce the mainstay of kitchens and menus again.

How can you tell what is in season?

Eating with the seasons means eating with the local conditions. Your favourite fruit or vegetable is always in season somewhere in the world, but that doesn't mean you should eat it all year round. Different seasons can be experienced within a single country or region as well. What might be in season in the north, might not be in season in the south.

SO HOW CAN YOU TELL WHAT'S LOCAL, AND WHAT'S IN SEASON?

✪ **GOOGLE IT!** If you are planning your weekly meals and writing your shopping list, this is the perfect opportunity to do a quick search of your local produce market online to determine what is in season. You can then build your meal plan around this produce.

✪ **LOOK FOR PRODUCE THAT IS IN ABUNDANCE.** Produce with multiple varieties or in large quantities is usually in season.

✪ **COMPARE COST.** Seasonal produce will be cheaper than if you were to buy the same item at another time of year. It is much cheaper to get something from down the road than it is to import it from the other side of the world.

✪ **ASK YOUR LOCAL GREENGROCER FOR ADVICE.** If they are selling fresh produce it is fair to expect that they know what is in season, affordable and tasting great. They can probably also tell you when and where the produce was sourced.

If you follow these simple tips, cooking with the seasons will soon become second nature. To help get you started, we've divided this book into seasonal chapters. We've included a list of in-season fruits and vegetables at the start of each chapter, and designed each recipe around seasonal fruits and vegetables.

FACTORS IN SELECTING SEASONAL PRODUCE

Good food should be fun, affordable, enjoyed by everyone and most of all taste delicious. As well as thinking about the seasonality of produce, here are some other factors to keep in mind.

Fresh versus frozen

People frequently ask us for our opinion regarding whether fresh or frozen is better. The answer depends on what you mean by 'better'. Frozen vegetables are a convenient solution when you don't have time to get to the grocery store. Frozen produce is usually frozen immediately after harvesting and consequently it deteriorates slower and retains much of its nutrition and flavour, compared to fresh foods, which may lose nutrition and flavour during transit or which may have been picked early to assist with transportation and consequently were never given the opportunity to develop their full complement of nutrition and flavour.

One drawback of frozen fruits and vegetables, though, is their texture. When cooked, they tend to be much more soft and almost 'waterlogged' compared to cooking with fresh fruits and vegetables.

Fresh, seasonal and local produce is allowed to grow in its optimal conditions for longer, resulting in highly nutritious and flavoursome fruits and vegetables. The transit period is short, the deterioration is minimal, the effect on the environment is much less and the produce is much more versatile in terms of its potential uses.

Ultimately, it depends how you are using it. If something is in season, fresh is best as it is highly nutritious and versatile. If it is out of season and texture doesn't matter (such as in a smoothie), then frozen is a good option.

Organic produce

This is one area of great contention. Understanding what 'organic' means is actually quite difficult as there is no clear definition. Generally speaking, organic produce refers to produce that is free from synthetic pesticides.

It has been suggested that organic produce contains more nutrition, is better for the environment, better for children, tastes better and is less harmful to our health. However, there's actually no significant difference in the nutrition content of organic and non-organic food. In fact, most of the time, organic marketing techniques focus on scare campaigns rather than providing valid, scientifically supported evidence regarding the advantages of organic produce.

Food business is big business (because we all eat!). Just because one product claims to be organic, does not mean that others are not. Organic labelling is completely voluntary. Privately run organisations certify products as being organic—usually based on a set of criteria they have developed themselves, while adhering to minimum industry standards. So it is actually possible that organic certification companies have different certification standards.

As you can see, the organic food industry is a bit of a minefield. So what should you buy?

While from a nutrition perspective, organic produce is not significantly different from non-organic produce, from a practical perspective there can be substantial differences. Non-organic often lasts longer, is more affordable and much more readily available. In contrast, organic foods have shorter shelf lives, cost substantially more and can be difficult to find, not to mention the fact that you may not even know 'how organic' something is.

Considering that two of the major barriers to people regularly consuming fresh fruits and vegetables are time and cost, we strongly encourage people to consume fruits and vegetables in any way they can, and we would never discourage people from consuming non-organic produce. Fresh food shouldn't be about elitism, everyone should enjoy it. Scientifically developed pesticides have played an important role in improving the food production system to ensure that people around the world have access to healthy, fresh food.

With that said, if you strongly believe in organic produce, can afford it and you are organised enough to purchase it regularly, then go ahead. You're not doing yourself any harm, but know your certification logos! Check what standards the certifier has for organic produce before you assume anything.

In the end, just choose fresh, seasonal produce, organic or not, and if you're concerned wash your fruits and vegetables thoroughly.

'SUPERFOODS'

Now is probably a good opportunity to tackle the issue of 'superfoods'. Let's start by appreciating that there is no such thing as a superfood, and this is a term created by marketing executives in an attempt to get the edge over their competitors' product. In fact, we are almost at a point of 'superfood saturation', as more and more food producers try to label their products as superfoods and the credibility associated with the term diminishes.

It is also important to recognise that other foods not labelled superfoods may also be nutrient-rich and contain strong health benefits. Like the humble kiwi fruit, orange, apple, tomato, avocado, walnut and the list goes on … Unfortunately, now, more than ever, these food items which have been a staple of our lives for many years (and are closely linked to the health benefits enjoyed by some of the healthiest populations in the world), need to reinvent themselves to keep up with obscure, expensive and heavily marketed products, and sometimes non-scientifically supported products that will probably be superseded by others in a few months' time.

As we have already explained, there is no one food that can provide you with all of your nutritional requirements. A superfood is typically a food with higher levels of a specific nutrient, but it's not a magic bullet! No one food will make you healthy, cure your illness or do anything that sounds too good to be true! In fact, an over-reliance on superfoods may displace the consumption of other nutritious foods that contribute important nutrients to your diet.

One final word on superfoods. Sure some of these foods may have some good nutritional qualities, however, just as the term 'organic' can create an attitude towards food that is segregating and unsustainable, so too can superfoods. The relentless promotion of superfoods leaves many people feeling insecure if they don't enjoy or can't afford cold-pressed green smoothies or organic coconut water that has been sustainably sourced by hand from an exotic jungle in Thailand and transported up the tallest mountain by local farmers. It leaves people questioning whether their 'normal' diet is actually healthy and whether what they are feeding their family is appropriate.

Good food and good health should not be just for the rich and famous, and does not require raw organic leaf extract from a specific region of the Amazon rainforest. All it takes is a variety of fresh, seasonal fruits and vegetables, lean meats, whole grains and dairy. Good food should be fun, affordable, delicious and enjoyed by everyone!

THE ADVANTAGE OF HOME COOKING

This cookbook is designed to inspire you to cook at home—to help you enjoy cooking, and to make it easy. Most of the recipes in this cookbook are meals we think you can prepare on any average weeknight.

To us, home cooking is fundamental to good health and very important for social and family development. We both enjoy cooking, we find it fun, relaxing and we enjoy putting a smile on other people's faces by the meals we create, but we know that not everyone feels the same way.

Having said that, even if you don't enjoy cooking as much as we do, there are many other factors that might ignite the cook inside you! Here are just a few:

- Home cooking is more affordable than dining out or purchasing takeaway.
- Cooking a variety of meals at home helps you become more aware of the ingredients you consume and can result in better informed food choices.
- You are able to adjust recipes according to your personal taste.
- You are able to adjust recipes according to health requirements.
- Home cooks consume significantly less energy, saturated fat and salt than those who eat out regularly.
- You are able to use healthier ingredients, such as olive oil instead of vegetable oil.
- It can be relaxing and therapeutic.
- It can help the whole family develop healthy habits and attitudes towards food.
- It promotes positive social interactions between family members and friends.

TO US, HOME COOKING IS FUNDAMENTAL TO GOOD HEALTH AND VERY IMPORTANT FOR SOCIAL AND FAMILY DEVELOPMENT.

Increasing your fruit and vegetable intake in home-cooked meals

When you ask your friends, partner or family what they would like for dinner, what is the response? In most households the answer usually begins with a protein, for example 'chicken', or 'lamb chops'. This is a very dated approach to cooking and results in vegetables being included in the meal as an afterthought, out of obligation rather than enjoyment.

Well, it's time to flip that attitude upside down. With the price and carbon footprint of meats increasing, lean animal-based proteins can no longer be considered the hero of our dinner plates. We need to make vegetables the stars of our meals. This will assist us to reduce our meat portion sizes, and will ultimately improve our health, the environment and our back pocket!

SO HOW CAN YOU INCLUDE MORE FRUITS AND VEGETABLES IN YOUR DAILY INTAKE? WELL, FOR STARTERS:

✪ **SHOP WITH THE SEASONS.** Your produce will last longer, be more affordable and taste better, and if it tastes great it has more chance of being eaten.

✪ **PREPARE FRUITS AND VEGETABLES WHEN YOU HAVE TIME AND LEAVE THEM IN YOUR FRIDGE.** A bowl of diced watermelon is more likely to get eaten than a whole one sitting on the bench.

✪ **MAKE YOUR VEGETABLES INTERESTING.** Roasted sweet potato, braised leek, chilli green beans sound, look and are delicious. Include some nuts, use fresh herbs, the possibilities are endless.

✪ **BE CREATIVE. INCORPORATE FRUITS INTO SAVOURY MEALS.** Fresh fruit provides colour and acidity in salads, dried fruit adds texture and sweetness to grain-based dishes and cooked fruit adds a depth of flavour and warmth to main meals and desserts. Pear is a perfect example of this—throw some in a pan with your potatoes for roasting, or try caramelised pear with radicchio, walnuts, blue cheese and rocket (arugula) tossed together in a salad.

✪ **PREPARE, PLAN AND PRIORITISE.** Prepare a menu and shopping list and allocate a set time to do a weekly shop. Be realistic about your commitments and know when you will have time to prepare lengthy meals and when you need quick simple dishes. Use time-saving utensils such as graters or mandolines, and don't be afraid to purchase pre-chopped vegetables. Finally, invest in further education, for example, learning how to use a knife properly can save you a lot of time in the kitchen.

Shopping efficiently

Most of us enjoy eating, some of us enjoy cooking, but very few of us enjoy grocery shopping! Unfortunately, shopping is a means to an end. We meet so many people who simply don't eat well due to poor planning and prioritising—stemming largely from their unwillingness to shop. Shopping is important, and doing it correctly will save you time and money, and will help ensure you have a healthy, balanced and varied diet.

✪ **WRITE A SHOPPING LIST.** Base this on a weekly menu and on the seasonal produce available. Don't forget to include a little extra fruit and vegetables for snacking and lunch. If it's not there, you won't eat it—so buy it!

✪ **ORDER YOUR SHOPPING LIST.** Break your shopping list into dry products, refrigerated products and fresh fruits and vegetables. This will save you a lot of time, reduce impulse purchases and save you money.

✪ **SHOP AT THE DELI SECTION.** You can buy the exact amount of whatever you need, which will save you money and reduce wastage.

✪ **AVOID THE SUPERMARKET CONGA.** Don't aimlessly wander up and down every aisle in the supermarket. The fresh, healthy products in a supermarket are located around the perimeter of the store. Stick to these areas and only venture into the middle if you have a list.

✪ **STAY FOCUSED.** Having a shopping list helps reduce the 'Gruen Effect' that supermarkets try to create. That split second when the store's intentionally confusing layout makes your head spin, eyes glaze over and shoulders droop. It's the moment when you forget what you came for, give in and impulsively buy things you never knew you needed. The moment when a five-minute trip to the shops for bread and milk turns into a $59 purchase.

PURCHASING RED MEAT

For red meat such as beef and lamb to develop flavour and become tender, it must be hung. If meat is bright red and looks wet, it hasn't been hung properly. It should not be resting in a pool of juices or smell 'meaty'. Meat should be dark red in colour and appear almost dry. 'Marbling' refers to thin visible ribbons of intramuscular fat. Well-marbled meat tends to be expensive due to selective breeding, and extra care and time taken to raise and feed the cattle on, which is typically grains and corn, rather than grass, but can really include anything that the farmer feels will add flavour. Some farmers even add red wine to the feed of their cattle. The marbling inside red meat melts when cooked, adding a rich deep flavour and keeping the meat juicy and tender. However, due to its high fat content marbled meat is less healthy than lean meat and should be consumed as a treat! Contrary to popular belief, wagyu does not refer to marbled meat; rather it translates to 'Japanese beef' and can apply to any of several breeds of cattle with particular Japanese bloodlines.

SECONDARY CUTS ARE OFTEN MORE AFFORDABLE, BUT THIS IS DUE MORE TO DEMAND THAN QUALITY.

WHICH CUT OF MEAT?

Meats are classified as primary and secondary cuts. Primary cuts are not 'better' than secondary cuts, they just have different uses. The type of dish you are preparing will determine the most appropriate cut of meat for you to use.

Primary cuts generally refer to lean cuts of meat, such as fillet steak or chicken breast, and are generally cooked quickly, using techniques such as grilling (broiling) or pan-frying. Secondary cuts refer to those that usually contain more connective tissue and are often from load-bearing areas of the animal, for example shanks or shoulders. Secondary cuts take longer to prepare and require specialised cooking techniques, such as slow cooking. Secondary cuts are often more affordable, but this is due more to demand than quality.

PURCHASING CHICKEN

Chicken is one of the most commonly purchased proteins in the world. The conditions of chicken farming have been heavily publicised in recent years with many consumers becoming much more informed and consequently making the conscious decision to select free-range chicken.

When selecting chicken look for a bird without ripped or torn skin. The skin can vary from cream to yellow depending on the diet of the chicken, with yellow tones generally indicating corn-fed chicken. Where possible, rather than purchasing only a specific cut, such as chicken breast, purchase a whole chicken. For practically the same price as two breasts you receive two breasts, two thighs, two drumsticks, two wings and a carcass to use for making stock.

WHERE POSSIBLE, BUY SEAFOOD FROM TUESDAY TO SATURDAY—AS RETAILERS DON'T OFTEN RECEIVE SEAFOOD DELIVERIES OVER THE WEEKEND.

PURCHASING SEAFOOD

We often speak to people who dislike fish. When we ask why this is the case, the most common response is that they don't like the smell. Fish should not smell 'fishy'; rather, it should smell like the ocean. Always buy the freshest fish possible. If this is not possible, buy frozen fish which is filleted and frozen within hours of being caught, locking in the fresh flavour and nutrition and preventing deterioration.

Seafood is very delicate compared to other proteins, so buy seafood that is well presented and carefully handled and laid out. Fish should look moist, but not wet or slimy. If the fish is whole, the eyes should look full, not sunken, and the gills should be bright red. When you press the fish gently it should bounce back quickly. Fish fillets should be in one piece and not falling apart, and should look bright and not grey (oxidised). Unpeeled crustaceans should have all of the shell and legs attached.

WHICH FISH?

Fish is incredibly versatile—for example, any white fish can usually be replaced by another similarly sized white fish, and ocean trout and salmon are common substitutes for each other. Unless a dish explicitly requires a specific type of fish, choose what looks the best and most fresh on the day or whichever fish is the most affordable at the time. When choosing a fish, consider how thick or thin it is and therefore how long it will take to cook, and whether this is appropriate for the recipe you are cooking. If you still can't decide, don't be afraid to ask your fishmonger.

FARMED VERSUS WILD

Sustainable fish farming practices have been a topic of discussion in recent years. With the world's marine stocks at an all-time low and seafood recognised as such an important healthy food for future generations, our oceans and marine life must be protected. Some fish are farmed, hence a consistent supply is usually available. Other fish are caught in the wild and the supply is less predictable. How fish in the wild are caught determines how sustainable these fishing practices are. 'Super trawlers', for example, have a huge impact on the ecosystem because they decimate fish stocks indiscriminately.

Farmed fish, in contrast, are kept within a certain area and fed until they reach their optimal size. Many people suggest that wild fish are more nutritious than farmed fish as they feed off the ocean's natural food supply. There is little sound evidence to support this and as the quality of the feed given to farmed fish continues to improve, the nutrient differences become negligible. In fact, we could almost argue that the nutrition content and flavour of farmed fish will be more consistent because the feed is consistent.

So what seafood should we eat? Eat a variety of seafood (not just what's popular) to enjoy the nutritional benefits of all fish and crustaceans and to maintain our seafood stores for future generations.

PURCHASING FRUITS AND VEGETABLES

Fruits and vegetables naturally give us a variety of cues to indicate when they are ripe, including colour, smell and touch. Purchase fruit and vegetables that are well displayed and from grocery stores that are clean and tidy. Try not to worry so much about the shape, size or colour of fruits and vegetables, because just like us, they come in different shapes and sizes. If a fruit or vegetable is in season it is probably going to taste great irrespective of its appearance. As a society, we waste a huge amount of fresh produce that never even makes it to the shelves due to our selective nature and desire for what we think a perfect fruit or vegetable should look like. Worry less about looks and more about taste—just buy in season.

PURCHASING HERBS AND SPICES

We love herbs and spices and we aren't afraid to use them! Ground or whole, fresh or dried, sliced or diced, these ingredients are the key to quick flavour without excessive use of fats, sugars or salt.

Herbs, including basil, coriander (cilantro), thyme and sage can be purchased fresh or dried. Dried, they are more economical because they have a substantially longer shelf life compared to fresh herbs. Many people do not use fresh herbs because they can be expensive and spoil quickly. However, fresh herbs are versatile and can be used in a range of dishes to provide flavour, colour and freshness, so don't waste them! Use the leaves of herbs as a garnish or in salads, or finely dice the stems of soft herbs and use these like aromatic ingredients, for example, add basil stems to tomato-based pasta sauces.

Spices are affordable and available at most food retailers, and can be purchased whole or ground. Whole spices can be used to add texture as well as flavour. They also have a longer shelf life than ground spices—approximately 9–12 months compared to 3–6 months. Spices do not have use-by dates; however, the fresher they are the more flavoursome they will be.

Substituting ingredients

We love cooking, experimenting and having fun in the kitchen, and we want you to enjoy your time in the kitchen, too. Cooking shouldn't be stressful, and our recipes are certainly not designed to be followed to the letter. We don't over-complicate things, in fact quite the opposite—we're always on the lookout for time-saving, efficient ways to make healthy delicious food.

Similarly, we love when people take our recipes and adapt them to suit their own tastes or requirements. A recipe, particularly a savoury recipe, is merely a list of suggested ingredients cooked in a particular way. If, for one reason or another, you need to make a change or two, please go ahead. The recipes in this book are designed to be easy and achievable for you at home. They are yours to tweak and make your own.

CONSIDERATIONS WHEN SUBSTITUTING

That last paragraph comes with a disclaimer! When substituting an ingredient, try to understand what that particular ingredient brings to the dish. It could be texture: smooth, soft or crunchy. It could be colour. Or it could be flavour: sweet, salty or sour. When substituting an ingredient, please consider this first, as it will help you determine what the best substitution is.

Please also keep in mind that substituting ingredients may impact on the method slightly so, where possible, try to swap a like for a like. For example, if you don't want sliced pear in your salad and would prefer sliced peach, go ahead, this won't change the method. If you like your dressings a little more acidic, then add a little extra lemon juice, no problem! However, if you would like to swap calamari for pork fillet remember that pork will take longer to cook than calamari, so you will need to take this into account.

WE DON'T OVER-COMPLICATE THINGS ... WE'RE ALWAYS ON THE LOOKOUT FOR TIME-SAVING, EFFICIENT WAYS TO MAKE HEALTHY DELICIOUS FOOD.

When you substitute ingredients in dessert recipes, there is a little more science involved and a little more precision is required. Try not to adjust the base of dessert recipes too much—especially batters or mixtures that need to rise or set—but feel free to adjust their toppings and garnishes. For example, swap strawberries for blueberries or almonds for pepitas (pumpkin seeds). You could even add completely new and different components to a recipe, or mix and match recipes. Go ahead. We encourage it!

As you read this book you will notice we include suggested substitutions for all of our recipes. Our aim is to get you thinking about the process of cooking, and help you gain confidence in the kitchen. We also want you to think about adapting recipes to suit the seasons—a hearty pumpkin (winter squash) risotto can be just the thing on a cold winter's night, but if you replace the pumpkin with fresh peas then you can turn the dish into a celebration of spring!

NUTRITION

All of the recipes in *Quick.Easy.Healthy.* have been designed to be a nutritious and valuable part of a balanced diet.

Our savoury dishes, in most cases, provide a source of protein, carbohydrate and two to three serves of vegetables. And of course, we've also included some desserts. We don't believe in deprivation, we don't believe that sugar is evil. We believe in eating a balanced diet and enjoying a treat once in a while. By cooking our sweet recipes you will hopefully learn to appreciate what goes into desserts (and our desserts show a lot of restraint!), and the importance of portion control. Finally, we always try to ensure that our desserts are delicious and also nutritious in some way, whether that is from the inclusion of fruit, nuts, seeds or dairy you will also be getting some nutritional benefit.

Nutrition analysis

Every recipe comes complete with a nutritional analysis, so please use this information to make an informed decision regarding whether the meal is appropriate for you or how you might be able to change it so that it fits your individual nutrition requirements.

EACH RECIPE CONTAINS THE FOLLOWING NUTRITIONAL INFORMATION, PER SERVE, WITH MOST RECIPES DESIGNED TO SERVE 4:

ENERGY: measured in kilojoules (kJ) and calories (cal)

PROTEIN: measured in grams (g)

SODIUM: measured in milligrams (mg)

FAT: measured in grams (g)

SATURATED FAT: measured in grams (g)

CARBOHYDRATE: measured in grams (g)

SUGAR: measured in grams (g)

FIBRE: measured in grams (g)

Food labels

NUTRITION INFORMATION SECTION

The nutrition information section of food labels is often located on the back of products and includes information such as the ingredients list and serving sizes.

INGREDIENTS LIST

All the ingredients in a product are listed in order of weight from highest to lowest. The ingredients list must also detail the percentage of any main characterising ingredients of a product, for example, the percentage of apple in an apple muffin.

NUTRITION INFORMATION PANEL (NIP)

An NIP will include the quantity of a nutrient per serve and per 100 g. When comparing products, always compare their nutrient content per 100 g. This will give you an accurate comparison tool. Avoid comparing products per serve as the serving size of a product is 'recommended' and set by the producer. Consequently, two similar products can have different serving sizes.

THE NUTRITION INFORMATION PANEL MUST DISPLAY

- The number of serves per package.
- The average serving size.
- The average quantity of energy, protein, fat, saturated fat, carbohydrate, sugar and sodium per serve and per 100 g (or another unit).
- The name and the average quantity of any nutrient or substance which has been mentioned in a claim by the product.

Nutrition information panels provide important information regarding the nutrient content of a particular product. The NIP is not a claim, it is not subjective, it is fact. The NIP provides you with information regarding your actual nutrient intake from a product. When reading NIPs you need to be able to interpret the figures and understand whether the figures are high or low or appropriate for consumption based on your individual health status. Below is a guide to assist with this, and to provide some recommendations around what to look for in food products. It provides some general rules to determine if a product is healthy.

NUTRITION INFORMATION – EXAMPLE

SERVES PER PACK – 6
SERVING SIZE – 35 g

	Avg per serve	Avg per 100 g
ENERGY (kJ)	534 kJ	1524 kJ
PROTEIN (g)	2.1 g	6 g
FAT (g)		
– TOTAL	5.1 g	14.6 g
– SATURATED	0.5 g	1.4 g
CARBOHYDRATE (g)	13.9 g	39.8 g
– TOTAL SUGARS	4.5 g	12.8 g
SODIUM (mg)	23 mg	67 mg
DIETARY FIBRE (g)	10.6 g	30.2 g

WHAT TO LOOK FOR IN YOUR NIP:

- Total fat—look for less than 10 g per 100 g
- Saturated fat—look for less than 3 g per 100 g
- Sodium—look for less than 120 mg per 100 g
- Dietary fibre—look for more than 4 g per 100 g

NOTE

- **FRUIT WILL OFTEN BE HIGH IN SUGAR (FRUCTOSE)**
  This is okay and an exception to the low-sugar rule. Fruit is low in energy, low in fat, low in sodium and high in fibre, so a little extra natural sugar is reasonable. There are not many healthier and more convenient snacks!
- **CEREALS** Look for breakfast cereals with greater than 7 g per 100 g dietary fibre

ENERGY This is most commonly measured in kilojoules, with 4.2 kJ equating to approximately one calorie. The average healthy individual who regularly engages in moderate-intensity exercise should consume around 8700 kJ per day.

As a rule of thumb aim for around 2000 kJ at main meals and around 600–900 kJ per snack.

MACRONUTRIENTS PROVIDE ENERGY. THE FOUR MACRONUTRIENTS IN THE HUMAN DIET ARE:

- Fat (all forms), which provides 37 kJ per gram
- Alcohol, which provides 29 kJ per gram
- Protein, which provides 17 kJ per gram
- Carbohydrate, which provides 16 kJ per gram.

The consumption of more energy (kilojoules) than we require results in weight gain. It does not matter which nutrient this energy comes from. Whether these excess kilojoules come from carbohydrate, protein, fat or alcohol, they are all the same, and will result in weight gain.

At this stage we need to point out that just because a product is low in one nutrient (i.e. fat) it does not automatically mean that the same product is high in another nutrient (i.e. sugar). This is a very unfair consumer perception. There are many products commercially available that are indeed healthier than others and do not attempt to 'trick' consumers by claiming to be healthier in one area but unhealthy in another. Rather than being unfairly sceptical, consumers need to read NIPs and make an informed decision.

Food claims

'Nutrition information panels' and nutrition 'food claims' are two very different things. The information found in an NIP refers to the actual nutrient content of the product. Food claims are voluntary statements that can appear on the front of food labels and in advertising. They can be categorised as 'health claims' and 'nutrient content claims'.

Health claims

Health claims refer to a nutrition property of a product or a health outcome. There are two levels of health claims—'general' and 'high'. General-level health claims refer to general relationships between the nutrient content of a food and health, for example, 'protein keeps you full'. High-level health claims refer to how the nutrient content of a food can impact serious disease or be an indicator of serious disease, for example, 'plant sterols are proven to lower cholesterol and reduce risk of heart disease'. Food Standards Australia and New Zealand (FSANZ) who develop and administer the Australia New Zealand Food Standards Code, which lists requirements for foods such as additives, food safety and labelling, has a set of general health claims that companies are approved to use. If a company chooses to use another claim they must be able to support this with scientific evidence. FSANZ also has a set of 'food–health relationship claims' that are approved for use. If a company chooses to use a non-approved high-level health claim then they must be able to scientifically support this claim.

A food company is only able to make a health claim provided their product meets the Nutrient Profiling Scoring Criterion (NPSC). The NPSC refers to a score given to a product to determine if it is healthy. A score is determined based on the amount of energy, saturated fat, total sugars and sodium in the food, along with the amount of fruit, vegetables, nuts, legumes, and, in some cases, dietary fibre and protein. The NPSC ensures that products that are generally unhealthy cannot make health claims.

It is important to remember that health claims are voluntary. Just because a product does not have any health claims, does not mean it is not healthy. Furthermore, while FSANZ has a strict set of approved nutrition claims that food companies can use, a company is free to use another health claim, provided they can support this claim with scientific evidence. This can result in much more vague, suggestive and on occasions misleading claims—claims that are so vague, they are easy to support and difficult to disprove. For example, health products that may claim to 'clear skin when taken in conjunction with a healthy diet and exercise'. These claims are difficult to disprove, so they are not technically in breach of food-labelling standards.

Nutrient content claims

Nutrient content claims refer directly to the nutrient content of a product, and are legitimate, factual claims—for example, a claim that a product is a good source of fibre. FSANZ has specific criteria that products must meet to be able to make such claims. Below is an extensive list of nutrient content claims. Some of these claims may surprise you, but they certainly highlight the importance of understanding nutrient content claims in terms of being able to make informed food choices.

REDUCED

The food contains at least 25% less of the stated nutrient than in the same quantity of another similar product produced by the manufacturer.

INCREASED

The food contains at least 25% more of the stated nutrient than in the same quantity of another similar product produced by the manufacturer. In the case of fibre, the reference food must have at least 2 g of fibre per serve.

FREE FROM (for example, 'fat free')

The product cannot contain any of the stated nutrient in the claim.

PERCENTAGE FREE (for example, '97% fat free')

The product cannot contain more than 3% fat (3 g fat per 100 g).

CHOLESTEROL

Low The food contains no more cholesterol than:
(a) 10 mg per 100 ml for liquid food; or
(b) 20 mg per 100 g for solid food.

DIETARY FIBRE

Good source A serving of the food contains at least 4 g of dietary fibre.
Excellent source A serving of the food contains at least 7 g of dietary fibre.

ENERGY

Low The average energy content of the food is no more than:
(a) 80 kJ per 100 mL for liquid food; or
(b) 170 kJ per 100 g for solid food.
Diet (i) The average energy content of the food is no more than 80 kJ per 100 ml for liquid food or 170 kJ per 100 g for solid food, or
(ii) The food contains at least 40% less energy than in the same quantity of reference food.

FAT

Low fat (total)
The food contains no more fat than:
(a) 1.5 g per 100 ml for liquid food; or
(b) 3 g per 100 g for solid food.
Low saturated fat and trans fatty acids
The food contains no more saturated and trans fatty acids than:
(a) 0.75 g per 100 ml for liquid food; or
(b) 1.5 g per 100 g for solid food.

SALT OR SODIUM

Low The food contains no more sodium than: 120 mg per 100 ml for liquid food or 100 g for solid food.
No added The food contains no added sodium compound, including no added salt.

SUGAR OR SUGARS

Low The food contains no more sugars than:
(a) 2.5 g per 100 ml for liquid food; or
(b) 5 g per 100 g for solid food.
No added
(a) The food contains no added sugars, including as honey, malt or malt extracts; and
(b) The food contains no added concentrated fruit juice or deionised fruit juice.
Unsweetened
(a) The food meets the conditions for a nutrition content claim about no added sugar; and
(b) The food contains no intense sweeteners, sorbitol, mannitol, glycerol, xylitol, isomalt, maltitol or lactitol.

GLUTEN

Low The food contains no more than 20 mg gluten per 100 g of the food.

LACTOSE

Low The food contains no more than 2 g of lactose per 100 g of the food.

PROTEIN

Good source The food contains at least 10 g of protein per serve.

GLYCAEMIC INDEX

Low The numerical value of the glycaemic index of the food is 55 or below.
Medium The numerical value of the glycaemic index of the food is at least 56 and not exceeding 69.
High The numerical value of the glycaemic index of the food is 70 or above.

VITAMIN OR MINERAL (NOT INCLUDING POTASSIUM OR SODIUM)

Good source A serving of the food contains no less than 25% of the recommended daily intake for that vitamin or mineral.

BALANCE
AND VARIETY

Now that you are able to read food labels more confidently you will no doubt be a little shocked by the nutrient profile of some of your favourite foods. Don't panic. It's actually very unlikely that every food you eat will meet all of the guidelines detailed on pages 24–27.

Simply aim to consume a varied diet with plenty of different coloured fruits and vegetables along with small amounts of whole grains, dairy, lean meats and legumes spread over the day, and you will give yourself the best opportunity to meet your daily requirements and reduce risk of illness and disease. And if you master just a handful of the recipes in this book, you will certainly be on the right track.

And by reading and understanding food labels you will recognise when your intake of certain nutrients may be high and others low and you will be in a much better position to balance your intake over the day or week.

AIM TO CONSUME A VARIED DIET WITH DIFFERENT COLOURED FRUITS AND VEGETABLES ALONG WITH WHOLE GRAINS, DAIRY, LEAN MEATS AND LEGUMES.

WHY NOT TO DIET!

As you may have noticed, we don't diet. We enjoy all types of food. We are well aware of what we put into our bodies and we make informed choices. We don't classify foods as 'good' or 'bad', 'super' or 'evil', just foods we should eat more regularly than others.

Society is now beginning to recognise the relationship between food and health. What's important is to aim to consume a fresh, healthy and varied diet to assist in leading a healthy and happy life. But food isn't just medicine. Food needs to be fun. It's a part of our culture and it helps bring people together. It makes us happy, it forms an important part of socialising and it is a way for people to show support or a kind gesture.

We believe that fresh, quality food is delicious and healthy. We believe in enjoying good food with friends and family. We don't believe in diets.

Diets don't work because:

- Humans love food
- Humans love variety
- Humans hate rules
- Humans always want what they can't have!

Diets are a set of strict rules that:

- Do not take into account people's lifestyles
- Do not take into account people's personalities
- Do not take into account people's likes and dislikes
- Do not change behaviour by improving understanding.

Because of these reasons diets are not sustainable.

So throw those diet books away. Instead, understand where your food comes from and the importance of seasonal produce. Recognise that a healthy lifestyle involves a varied diet with lots of fruits and vegetables, a variety of dairy, grains and legumes, and a mixture of carbohydrates, proteins and good fats. Above all, remember that food should be fun. So pick a quick, easy, healthy recipe from this book, get into the kitchen and give it a go!

TEN TIPS FOR STRESS-FREE HEALTHY FOOD

1 Plan your meals—choose quick meals for busy days and nights and save meals requiring more preparation for when you have the time.

2 Shop regularly—develop a routine, choose a day and prioritise this day.

3 Pre-chop fruits and vegetables and leave these in your fridge for use when required.

4 Always keep some frozen vegetables in the freezer.

5 Use herbs and spices for quick and easy flavour.

6 Prepare healthy snacks in bulk, such as vegetable frittatas or savoury muffins.

7 Prepare meals ahead—slow-cooked meals, curries, stews and soups all store well and are perfect for freezing.

8 Cook versatile meals, for example bolognese sauce that can also be used in bakes or chilli con carne.

9 Clean as you go—nobody likes dishes. Stay on top of them!

10 Delegate—ask everyone in the house to roll up their sleeves and pitch in. It could be as simple as boiling the pasta or warming the oven.

SIX BEHAVIOURS FOR HEALTHY LIVING

1. DRINK PLENTY OF WATER.

2. EAT AT LEAST FIVE SERVES OF VEGETABLES A DAY.

3. EAT MINDFULLY—EAT SLOWLY, SAVOUR AND ENJOY YOUR FOOD.

4. EAT REGULARLY AND DO NOT SKIP MEALS.

5. PRIORITISE MEAL PLANNING, SHOPPING AND COOKING.

6. EXERCISE DAILY.

SUMMER

LIGHT. BRIGHT. SWEET.

It's time to get outside, hit the beach, fill our bodies with vitamin D and charge up those barbecues. Summer food is all about grills, vibrant salads and fruity desserts. It's about being spontaneous and casual, and enjoying lots of fresh, light and delicious food with friends and family in the park, by the pool or by the sea. Summer is all about sunshine, food and people.

The summer recipes in this chapter make great use of beautiful seafood, sweet summer fruits, sweet juicy tomatoes and crunchy refreshing cucumbers. Our Greek lamb with watermelon, olive and mint salad (page 55) is quite simply summer on a plate.

SUMMER SHOPPING LIST

Summer fruits are a great example of seasonal produce. Because summer fruits are not available throughout the year we are excited by the first sight of peaches, plums, apricots and the many other sweet and bright summer fruits. Imagine if the humble pear or apple was only available in winter, we would probably regard these much higher than we currently do!

When buying summer fruits, look for those that are bright skinned, not too firm or too soft, free from visible bruises and that have been well displayed. Summer fruits are delicate, so be careful how you transport them.

Summer vegetables include eggplants, cucumbers, tomatoes, peas and beans, zucchini and much more. Summer vegetables should be firm, crisp and brightly coloured and are often best grilled or eaten fresh.

VEGETABLES

- ASPARAGUS
- BEAN SPROUTS
- BEETROOT (BEETS)
- BROCCOLI
- BUTTER BEANS
- CABBAGE
- CAPSICUMS
  (PEPPERS)
- CARROTS
- CAULIFLOWER
- CELERY
- CHILLIES
- CHOKOS
- CUCUMBERS
- EGGPLANT
  (AUBERGINES)
- FLAT BEANS
- GREEN BEANS
- LEEKS
- LETTUCE
- MUSHROOMS
- OKRA

- ONIONS
- PEAS
- POTATOES
- PUMPKIN
  (WINTER SQUASH)
- RADISH
- RHUBARB
- SNAKE
  (YARD-LONG)
  BEANS
- SNOW PEAS
  (MANGETOUT)
- SPRING ONIONS
  (SCALLIONS)
- SQUASH
- SUGAR SNAP PEAS
- SWEETCORN
- TOMATOES
- TURNIPS
- WATERCRESS
- ZUCCHINI
  (COURGETTES)

FRUIT

- APRICOTS
- AVOCADOS
- BANANAS
- BLACKBERRIES
- BLUEBERRIES
- CHERRIES
- FIGS
- GRAPES
- HONEYDEW
  MELON
- HOWELL PEARS
- LIMES
- LYCHEES
- MANGOES
- MANGOSTEENS
- NECTARINES
- PAPAYA

- PARADISE PEARS
- PASSIONFRUIT
- PEACHES
- PINEAPPLE
- PLUMS
- PRICKLY PEARS
- RAMBUTANS
- RASPBERRIES
- RED CURRANTS
- ROCKMELON
- STRAWBERRIES
- VALENCIA
  ORANGES
- WATERMELON
- WHITE
  CURRANTS
- WILLIAMS PEARS

SNAPPER CEVICHE WITH MANGO AND AVOCADO SALSA

SERVES 4

Ceviche is a method of preparing seafood by curing it in citrus juices. The combination of lemon, avocado, mango and coriander provides the perfect balance of sweet and sour married together by the smooth fats of the avocado.

400 g (14 oz) sashimi-grade snapper, skin removed
juice of 2 lemons
3 handfuls coriander (cilantro), leaves picked and reserved, stems finely chopped
1 green chilli, seeded and thinly sliced
4 tomatoes, diced
2 tablespoons olive oil
pinch of salt

MANGO AND AVOCADO SALSA
1 mango, diced
1 avocado, diced
3 spring onions (scallions), thinly sliced on an angle
1 Lebanese (short) cucumber, diced

Dice the snapper into 1 cm (½ inch) pieces and place in a bowl. Cover with three-quarters of the lemon juice and stir in the coriander stems and green chilli. Set aside for 15 minutes or until the fish turns white.

Place the tomato in a bowl with the olive oil and salt.

Combine the mango, avocado, spring onion, cucumber and reserved coriander leaves in a bowl and drizzle with the remaining lemon juice.

Pile the tomatoes onto four serving plates. Top with the snapper ceviche, then the mango and avocado salsa, and serve.

NUTRITION TIP *This dish is full of fats ... good fats though! Plenty of polyunsaturated and monounsaturated fats from the fish, avocado and olive oil. These fats help maintain a healthy heart, brain and eyes, they are anti-inflammatory and they assist in maintaining healthy cholesterol levels.*

SUBSTITUTION *If you don't like snapper, try another sashimi-grade fresh fish, such as salmon or tuna. And if you're unsure about selecting fish, refer to page 21 of this book or head to your local fish market or fresh seafood store and seek their expert advice.*

NUTRITION INFORMATION (PER SERVE)	ENERGY	PROTEIN	SODIUM	FAT	SAT FAT	CARBOHYDRATE	SUGAR	FIBRE
	1624 kJ (388 cal)	25.6 g	163 mg	24.3 g	4.9 g	13.6 g	12.8 g	6.8 g

TOMATO AND FETA FRITTATA WITH PLUM AND ZUCCHINI SALAD

MAKES 12 MUFFIN-SIZED FRITTATAS

A healthy snack, quick lunch or light dinner, these little treats are super simple, satisfying and nutritious. Enjoy them hot or cold with a side salad or something more.

olive oil spray, for greasing
3 handfuls basil, leaves picked and reserved for the salad, stems finely chopped
1 lemon
250 g (9 oz) cherry tomatoes, halved
¼ teaspoon chilli flakes (optional)
freshly ground black pepper, to taste
120 g (4¼ oz) feta cheese
10 eggs
80 ml (2½ fl oz/⅓ cup) low-fat milk

PLUM AND ZUCCHINI SALAD
2 zucchini (courgettes)
2 plums, thinly sliced
2 tablespoons olive oil

Preheat the oven to 200°C (400°F/Gas 6). Lightly grease a 12-hole regular muffin tray (or patty pan or similar), then line each muffin hole with a square of baking paper.

Put the basil stems in a bowl. Finely grate the lemon zest and add to the basil stems along with the cherry tomatoes, chilli flakes, if using, and black pepper. (Reserve the lemon to juice for the salad.) Stir to combine, then divide the tomato mixture between the lined muffin-tray holes and crumble a little feta over each.

Whisk the eggs and milk together in a large jug (pitcher). Carefully pour the egg mixture into each hole until equally divided. Bake for 15–20 minutes or until golden brown and puffy, then turn the frittatas out onto a wire rack to cool slightly.

Meanwhile, peel the zucchini into long, wide strips using a vegetable peeler. Place in a bowl with the plum slices, olive oil and basil leaves, and squeeze in the lemon juice.

Serve the frittatas with the plum and zucchini salad.

 NUTRITION TIP *With around 8 g of quality protein per frittata, two make a perfect post-exercise snack to help muscle recovery.*

SUBSTITUTION *In summer you could use roasted capsicum (pepper) or zucchini instead of cherry tomatoes; in autumn, spinach; winter, try diced roasted pumpkin; and in spring, peas or asparagus. In place of plums, try peach, nectarine or mango.*

NUTRITION INFORMATION (PER FRITTATA)	ENERGY 393 kJ (94 cal)	PROTEIN 7.8 g	SODIUM 173 mg	FAT 6.2 g	SAT FAT 2.9 g	CARBOHYDRATE 1.3 g	SUGAR 1.1 g	FIBRE 0.8 g

WHILE FRESH CORN GIVES THE BEST RESULT FROZEN CORN CAN BE USED INSTEAD. JUST TRY TO DRAIN THE CORN WELL SO THAT THE EXCESS WATER DOESN'T LEAVE THE FRITTERS SOGGY.

SWEET CORN FRITTERS WITH TOMATO AND AVOCADO SALSA

SERVES 4

Who doesn't love fritters? This vegie-packed dish is one the whole family will love. It's quick and easy, and can make a great Sunday brunch or a light dinner.

2 corn cobs, kernels removed
50 g (1¾ oz/⅓ cup) wholemeal (whole-wheat) self-raising flour
1 handful coriander (cilantro), stems and leaves (reserve some leaves for the salsa)
1 egg
pinch of chilli flakes
pinch of salt
1 teaspoon olive oil

TOMATO AND AVOCADO SALSA
250 g (9 oz) cherry tomatoes, halved
1 avocado, diced
¼ red onion, sliced as thinly as possible
1 tablespoon olive oil
1 tablespoon lime juice

Put half the corn kernels, the flour, coriander, egg, chilli flakes and salt in a small food processor and blitz to combine. Stir in the remaining corn.

Heat the olive oil in a non-stick frying pan over high heat. Add a quarter of the batter to the pan and cook for 1–2 minutes on each side or until golden brown and cooked through. Remove to a plate and use the remaining batter to make three more fritters.

Combine the cherry tomatoes, avocado, onion and remaining coriander leaves in a small bowl. Drizzle with the olive oil and the lime juice. Divide the fritters among four serving plates. Spoon over the salsa and serve immediately.

 NUTRITION TIP *Corn is a great source of insoluble fibre which is important for good bowel health. The corn in this meal also provides a valuable source of carbohydrate instead of more common carbohydrate sources such as breads and cereals.*

SUBSTITUTION *If you don't love coriander as much as us, then try parsley or basil.*

NUTRITION INFORMATION (PER SERVE)	ENERGY 1273 kJ (304 cal)	PROTEIN 7.9 g	SODIUM 70 mg	FAT 20.3 g	SAT FAT 4.2 g	CARBOHYDRATE 18.8 g	SUGAR 5.1 g	FIBRE 8.1 g

CHICKEN RATATOUILLE WITH ROCKET PESTO

SERVES 4

Ratatouille is the perfect way to use up some of those vegetables left over in the bottom of the crisper. It stores well and can be a great light lunch or a satisfying dinner when paired with a protein.

1½ tablespoons olive oil
1 brown onion, diced
1 small eggplant (aubergine), diced
4 garlic cloves, thinly sliced
2 zucchini (courgettes), diced
1 red capsicum (pepper), diced
1 tablespoon fennel seeds
800 g (1 lb 12 oz) tinned tomatoes
2 x 250 g (9 oz) boneless, skinless
    chicken breasts, cut into
    2 cm (¾ inch) dice
80 g (2¾ oz) feta cheese, to serve
crusty bread, toasted, to serve

ROCKET PESTO
3 handfuls basil, leaves picked
1 large handful rocket (arugula)
juice and zest of 1 lemon
2 tablespoons pine nuts
2 tablespoons olive oil

Heat the olive oil in a large saucepan or stockpot over high heat. Add the onion and cook, stirring, for 30 seconds or until translucent. Add the eggplant and cook for 3–4 minutes until it starts to soften, then add the garlic, zucchini and red capsicum. Stir in the fennel seeds, leave to toast for a moment, then add the tomatoes. Bring to the boil, then reduce the heat to medium and simmer for 15–20 minutes until the ratatouille thickens and the tomato sauce darkens in colour slightly. Add the chicken and cook for a further 3–4 minutes, stirring occasionally, until just cooked.

Meanwhile, combine half the basil, the rocket, lemon juice, lemon zest and pine nuts in a food processor and blitz until finely chopped. Stir in the olive oil.

Divide the ratatouille between bowls. Add a spoonful of rocket pesto to each of four bowls and crumble over the feta. Serve with a slice of toasted crusty bread.

NUTRITION TIP *Most people know that for good health we should aim for five serves of vegetables a day. This dish will go a long way towards helping you meet your vegetable requirements. It also stores well, meaning tomorrow's vegetables are sorted too!*

SUBSTITUTION *Ratatouille is a versatile side dish and can partner with a range of proteins. Try baked white fish, which will soak up the sauce and flavours of the ratatouille.*

NUTRITION INFORMATION (PER SERVE)	ENERGY	PROTEIN	SODIUM	FAT	SAT FAT	CARBOHYDRATE	SUGAR	FIBRE
	2382 kJ (569 cal)	40.8 g	629 mg	29.8 g	6.8 g	29.9 g	12.3 g	9.2 g

RARE TUNA WITH SOBA NOODLE, RADISH AND SESAME SALAD

SERVES 4

This Japanese-inspired dish is fresh and healthy. The crispy fresh salad complements the soft tender oily tuna perfectly.

2 x 200 g (7 oz) sashimi-grade
   tuna steaks
1 x 90 g (3¼ oz) packet soba noodles
2 handfuls snow peas (mangetout),
   trimmed and sliced
1 Lebanese (short) cucumber,
   cut into matchsticks
4 radishes, sliced as thinly as possible
1 tablespoon rice bran oil (or olive oil)
1 tablespoon sesame seeds (white
   or black, both work)

SOY AND SESAME DRESSING
2 tablespoons mirin
1 tablespoon light soy sauce
2 tablespoons rice wine vinegar
1 teaspoon sesame oil
1 thumb-sized piece ginger, grated

Combine all the soy and sesame dressing ingredients in a small bowl and stir. Place the tuna steaks in a shallow bowl or container. Pour about a third of the dressing over the tuna to form a quick marinade. Leave to rest for 5–10 minutes. Reserve the remaining dressing.

Meanwhile, blanch the soba noodles in a large saucepan of boiling water according to the packet directions. Add the snow peas for the final minute of cooking. Drain and refresh under a little cold water to stop the cooking process. Drain again, then tip the soba noodles and snow peas into a large mixing bowl. Add the cucumber, radish and reserved dressing, and gently combine. Set aside.

Heat the rice bran oil in a non-stick frying pan over high heat. Drain the tuna from the marinade and discard any leftover marinade. Add the tuna to the pan and cook for 1 minute on each side or until golden brown but very rare in the middle. Remove from the pan, rest for a minute, then slice into 5 mm (¼ inch) thick pieces.

Pile the soba noodle salad onto four serving plates, top with the tuna and sprinkle over the sesame seeds to serve.

 NUTRITION TIP *Tuna is a great source of omega-3 fatty acids which are important for reducing the risk of cardiovascular disease. One serve of this dish provides over 100% of your recommended daily omega-3 intake.*

SUBSTITUTION *Salmon or kingfish are perfect replacements for tuna in this dish.*

NUTRITION INFORMATION (PER SERVE)	ENERGY 1035 kJ (247 cal)	PROTEIN 31.4 g	SODIUM 480 mg	FAT 6.7 g	SAT FAT 0.9 g	CARBOHYDRATE 13.1 g	SUGAR 5.2 g	FIBRE 3.6 g

PRAWN, ICEBERG AND AVOCADO SLIDERS

MAKES 8
SLIDERS

We don't use iceberg lettuce very much, because we both usually enjoy the bitter contrast of greens such as rocket (arugula). However, it works a treat in this dish, providing a fresh crunch.

130 g (4½ oz/½ cup) low-fat
    Greek-style yoghurt
1 tablespoon olive oil
1 tablespoon dijon mustard
8 cornichons, thinly sliced
2 tablespoons capers, rinsed
1 handful dill, roughly chopped
zest and juice of 1 lemon
500 g (1 lb 2 oz) cooked prawns (shrimp)
⅛ iceberg lettuce, thinly sliced
1 avocado, thinly sliced
8 small wholemeal slider buns, halved
1 Lebanese (short) cucumber,
    thinly sliced

Stir together the yoghurt, olive oil, mustard, cornichons, capers, dill, lemon zest and juice in a large bowl. Cut the prawns into small pieces (about 1 cm/½ inch cubed) and stir through the yoghurt mixture.

Divide the avocado and iceberg among the slider buns. Top with the prawn mixture and cucumber, then serve.

 NUTRITION TIP *If you are gluten intolerant, convert this recipe to a salad and add 95 g (3¼ oz/½ cup) of cooked brown rice per serve for a nutritious source of carbohydrate.*

SUBSTITUTION *This dish works with just about any cooked seafood—white fish, salmon, crab or lobster ...*

NUTRITION INFORMATION (PER SLIDER)	ENERGY	PROTEIN	SODIUM	FAT	SAT FAT	CARBOHYDRATE	SUGAR	FIBRE
	1681 kJ (402 cal)	23.0 g	867 mg	12.5 g	2.9 g	45.2 g	11.8 g	7.2 g

TORN MOZZARELLA, PROSCIUTTO, PEACH AND ASPARAGUS SALAD

SERVES 4

Sweet yellow peaches, salty prosciutto and stretchy gooey mozzarella, do we really need to say any more? Take this delicious combination and add basil leaves, cherry tomatoes, asparagus and radish, and create not only a beautiful looking salad, but an absolutely scrumptious summer lunch.

4 thick slices sourdough bread,
    torn into bite-sized pieces
1 tablespoon olive oil, plus
    1 tablespoon extra
18 asparagus spears, cut into
    4 cm (1½ inch) lengths
2 tablespoons white wine vinegar
3 radishes, thinly sliced
2 French shallots, thinly sliced
2 yellow peaches, stones removed
    and thinly sliced
4 prosciutto slices, torn into strips
120 g (4¼ oz) fresh mozzarella,
    torn into bite-sized chunks
200 g (7 oz) cherry tomatoes, halved
3 handfuls basil, leaves picked

Preheat the oven to 180°C (350°F/Gas 4).

Scatter the torn bread over a baking tray and drizzle over 1 tablespoon of the olive oil. Transfer to the oven and cook, turning halfway, for 4–5 minutes until golden brown. Remove from the oven and set aside to cool.

Meanwhile, bring a saucepan of water to the boil over medium–high heat and add the asparagus. Cook for 2 minutes or until just tender, then drain and plunge the asparagus into a bowl of cold water to stop the cooking process. Drain again.

Combine the asparagus, remaining olive oil, vinegar, radish, French shallot, peach slices, prosciutto, mozzarella, cherry tomatoes, sourdough and half the basil leaves in a large bowl. Divide among serving plates, top with the remaining basil leaves and serve.

NUTRITION TIP *Prosciutto, like most cured meats, is high in salt. It's not the focus of this dish, just an ingredient. It provides a salty component and therefore no additional salt is necessary.*

SUBSTITUTION *Instead of peaches try nectarines, plums or mango.*

NUTRITION INFORMATION (PER SERVE)	ENERGY 1519 kJ (363 cal)	PROTEIN 20.1 g	SODIUM 819 mg	FAT 20.0 g	SAT FAT 7.0 g	CARBOHYDRATE 22.3 g	SUGAR 9.9 g	FIBRE 5.8 g

FISH TACOS WITH GUACAMOLE AND PINEAPPLE SALSA

SERVES 4

This is a great way to squeeze a little extra fish into your diet, and the whole family will love it! Mexican food should be fresh, healthy and fun. These tacos are tangy, sweet and smoky, and, of course, taste great!

PINEAPPLE SALSA

2 handfuls coriander (cilantro), leaves picked

3 spring onions (scallions), thinly sliced

4 radishes, finely julienned or grated

¼ pineapple, cored and cut into small dice

2 Lebanese (short) cucumbers, diced

juice of 1 lemon

1 teaspoon ground cumin

1 teaspoon smoked paprika

2 x 200 g (7 oz) white fish fillets, such as snapper

2 tablespoons olive oil

1 avocado

8 tortillas

⅛ purple cabbage, finely shredded

To make the pineapple salsa, combine the coriander leaves, spring onion, radish, pineapple and cucumber in a bowl. Squeeze over half the lemon juice. Stir to combine.

Preheat a non-stick frying pan over high heat. Combine the cumin and paprika in a small bowl and rub it over the fish, add the olive oil to the pan and cook the fish for 2–3 minutes on each side or until just cooked. Remove the fish and flake it with tongs.

Meanwhile, to make the guacamole, halve the avocado and remove the stone. Scrape out the flesh into a small food processor. Add the remaining lemon juice and blend to combine. Alternatively, mash the avocado with a fork, then mix in the juice.

Warm the tortillas in a microwave or low oven. Spread with guacamole, top with purple cabbage, flaked fish and pineapple salsa. Serve immediately.

 NUTRITION TIP *Coating seafood in spices adds flavour and a crunchy exterior similar to battered or crumbed seafood but without the fat from deep-frying. Try using whole spices or adding a few sesame seeds to the spice mixture for added crunch and nutrition.*

SUBSTITUTION *If fish just isn't going to get past fussy family members, then swap the fish for evenly diced pieces of chicken. For a vegetarian alternative, use diced tofu or kidney beans.*

NUTRITION INFORMATION (PER SERVE)	ENERGY 1705 kJ (407 cal)	PROTEIN 26.7 g	SODIUM 415 mg	FAT 20.9 g	SAT FAT 4.4 g	CARBOHYDRATE 23.8 g	SUGAR 8.9 g	FIBRE 8.5 g

OREGANO CHICKEN WITH SMOKY BABA GHANOUSH

SERVES 4

Along with its cool name, baba ghanoush is also delicious and really healthy. Eggplant, olive oil and tahini equals healthy fats and vegetables. The cucumber and onion provide a fresh crunch and the baba ghanoush a deep smoky flavour, which together complement the zesty chicken marinade.

1 tablespoon olive oil, plus
   1 tablespoon extra
2 x 250 g (9 oz) boneless, skinless
   chicken breasts, sliced
   1 cm (½ inch) thick
1 lemon
1 handful oregano leaves,
   roughly chopped
3 Lebanese (short) cucumbers,
   cut into bite-sized chunks
½ red onion, thinly sliced
3 tomatoes, cut into wedges
2 teaspoons sesame seeds

SMOKY BABA GHANOUSH
2 eggplants (aubergines)
1 tablespoon olive oil
2 tablespoons tahini
1 garlic clove, grated
2 teaspoons smoked paprika
zest and juice of 1 lemon

To make the baba ghanoush, preheat the oven to 230°C (450°F/Gas 8). Line a roasting tin with baking paper. Place the eggplants in the tin. Roast for 15–20 minutes until the eggplants are tender and the skin is charred. Remove from the oven and set aside to cool.

Cut the eggplants in half and scoop out the flesh into a food processor. Add the olive oil, tahini, garlic, paprika, lemon zest and juice, then blend until smooth. Transfer into a bowl and set aside.

Heat 1 tablespoon of the olive oil in a large frying pan over high heat. Add the chicken and cook for 2–3 minutes on each side until golden brown and just cooked through. While the chicken cooks, finely grate the lemon zest into a bowl and add the chopped oregano and remaining oil. Place the cooked chicken in the bowl and toss to coat.

Combine the cucumber, onion, tomato, sesame seeds and lemon juice in a large bowl.

Serve the chicken with the baba ghanoush and cucumber salad.

 NUTRITION TIP *Tahini is made from ground sesame seeds and provides a valuable source of polyunsaturated and monounsaturated fats and many vitamins and minerals.*

SUBSTITUTION *If fresh oregano is hard to find, use dried oregano or a dried spice mix, which usually includes thyme and rosemary as well.*

NUTRITION INFORMATION (PER SERVE)	ENERGY	PROTEIN	SODIUM	FAT	SAT FAT	CARBOHYDRATE	SUGAR	FIBRE
	1644 kJ (393 cal)	34.5 g	115 mg	21.3 g	3.3 g	11.5 g	11.0 g	9.2 g

HALOUMI WITH CORN, ZUCCHINI AND JALAPEÑO SAUCE

SERVES 4

This is a full-flavoured vegetarian dish that certainly won't leave you asking, 'Where is the meat?' This satisfying, colourful and textural dish is easy to prepare and delicious hot or cold.

1 tablespoon rice bran oil (or olive oil)
2 zucchini (courgettes), diced
4 corn cobs, kernels removed
   (or 200 g/7 oz/1⅓ cups frozen
   corn, defrosted)
2 teaspoons cumin seeds
1 long red chilli, thinly sliced
2 garlic cloves, crushed or
   finely chopped
½ red onion, thinly sliced
250 g (9 oz) cherry tomatoes, halved
200 g (7 oz) haloumi cheese,
   cut into 12 thin slices

JALAPEÑO SAUCE

2 tablespoons chopped jalapeño chillies
2 tablespoons chopped cornichons
3 handfuls coriander (cilantro)
juice of 1 lemon
1 tablespoon olive oil

To make the jalapeño sauce, combine the jalapeños, cornichons, coriander stems and leaves (reserve a handful of leaves for serving) and lemon juice in a small food processor and blend to combine. Stir in the olive oil and set aside.

Heat the rice bran oil in a large non-stick frying pan over high heat. Add the zucchini, corn kernels, cumin seeds, chilli and garlic, and cook for 2–3 minutes or until the corn is golden and tender. Transfer into a bowl and combine with the red onion and cherry tomatoes.

Add the haloumi to the pan and cook for 1–2 minutes until golden on both sides.

Divide the haloumi among four serving plates, add a dollop of jalapeño sauce, some corn and tomato salad, top with the reserved coriander leaves and serve.

NUTRITION TIP *Haloumi can be high in salt and fat. Don't make it the main part of the dish, instead mix it through the corn salad and allow it to complement the other ingredients.*

SUBSTITUTION *If you aren't a fan of spicy food, try removing the seeds and membrane from the red chilli. Of course you can remove the chilli completely—however, it adds extra flavour and colour, so rather than completely removing it consider using less. If haloumi isn't your thing, try grilled asparagus, prawns (shrimp) or scallops.*

NUTRITION INFORMATION (PER SERVE)	ENERGY 1454 kJ (347 cal)	PROTEIN 18.3 g	SODIUM 1473 mg	FAT 18.5 g	SAT FAT 6.9 g	CARBOHYDRATE 21.7 g	SUGAR 9.9 g	FIBRE 10.5 g

GREEK LAMB WITH WATERMELON, OLIVE AND MINT SALAD

SERVES 4

This beautiful watermelon, olive and mint salad is a great summer barbecue dish. The mint is refreshing and the olives add a salty contrast to the sweetness of the watermelon. Paired with our Greek-inspired lamb this is a fabulous summer entertaining dish.

2 lemons
130 g (4½ oz/½ cup) low-fat
   Greek-style yoghurt
2 garlic cloves, crushed
2 teaspoons dried oregano
2 tablespoons olive oil
500 g (1 lb 2 oz) lamb cutlets
   (or loin chops)

WATERMELON, OLIVE AND MINT SALAD

300 g (10½ oz) watermelon flesh, diced
55 g (2 oz/⅓ cup) pitted kalamata olives
2 Lebanese (short) cucumbers,
   cut into bite-sized chunks
1 small red onion, thinly sliced
2 handfuls mint, leaves picked
2 tablespoons olive oil
1 teaspoons dried oregano

Zest the two lemons into a small bowl and stir through the yoghurt. Season with salt and pepper to taste. Juice the lemons and set aside.

Combine the garlic, oregano, half the lemon juice and the olive oil in a shallow non-metallic bowl. Add the lamb and toss well to coat. Set aside while you make the salad.

Combine the watermelon, olives, cucumber, red onion and mint leaves in a salad bowl. Pour over the olive oil, remaining lemon juice and add the oregano. Toss gently to combine.

Preheat the grill (broiler), barbecue or a frying pan to high heat. Add the lamb and cook, basting with any leftover marinade, for 3–4 minutes on each side until cooked to your liking. Serve with the watermelon, olive and mint salad and the lemon zest yoghurt.

NUTRITION TIP *If you are extra hungry, don't turn to more meat. Bolster your vegetables instead. Increase the cucumber content of this salad or include tomatoes or perhaps try roasted capsicum (peppers).*

SUBSTITUTION *Grilled chicken breast is an easy substitution for the lamb, but just remember it will take a little longer than red meat to cook. If you are after a yoghurt alternative, cottage cheese or a natural soy yoghurt also work well.*

NUTRITION INFORMATION (PER SERVE)	ENERGY 1727 kJ (412 cal)	PROTEIN 31.3 g	SODIUM 339 mg	FAT 23.7 g	SAT FAT 5.9 g	CARBOHYDRATE 16.5 g	SUGAR 14.7 g	FIBRE 4.5 g

JAMAICAN CHICKEN WITH CHARRED CORN SALAD

SERVES 4

We love spices and we aren't afraid to use them! This dish uses readily available spices and familiar ingredients to produce a dish that even the most critical family members will enjoy.

4 x 100 g (3½ oz) boneless, skinless chicken thighs
1 tablespoon rice bran oil (or olive oil)
4 corn cobs, kernels removed (or 200 g/7 oz/1½ cups frozen corn, defrosted)
¼ pineapple, cored and diced
4 spring onions (scallions), sliced thinly on an angle
2 Lebanese (short) cucumbers, seeded and diced
large handful basil, leaves picked
1 lemon

JAMAICAN RUB
1 teaspoon allspice
2 teaspoons ground coriander
1 teaspoon light brown sugar
2 teaspoons onion powder
¼ teaspoon salt flakes

To make the Jamaican rub, stir all the ingredients together in a bowl.

Rub the chicken with the Jamaican rub on all sides. Heat the rice bran oil in a non-stick frying pan over medium–high heat. Add the chicken and cook for 2–3 minutes on each side until cooked through. Remove the chicken from the pan and set aside, lightly covered, on a plate. Add the corn kernels to the pan and cook for 1–2 minutes until golden and slightly charred.

Meanwhile, combine the pineapple, spring onion, cucumber and basil leaves in a bowl. Halve the lemon, then squeeze the juice into the bowl and stir to combine.

Stir the corn through the salad and divide among four serving plates. Place a piece of chicken on top and serve.

 NUTRITION TIP *Squeeze an extra serve of vegetables into this meal by adding some halved cherry tomatoes. In summer they provide a lovely colour and beautiful burst of freshness to the dish.*

SUBSTITUTION *This spice mix is delicious and works with many proteins. Try it on pork or even tofu.*
If you want to reduce the total fat content of this meal, try using chicken breast. Just be aware though, that it is a little less forgiving than thigh and can dry out if overcooked.

NUTRITION INFORMATION (PER SERVE)	ENERGY	PROTEIN	SODIUM	FAT	SAT FAT	CARBOHYDRATE	SUGAR	FIBRE
	1729 kJ (413 cal)	29.9 g	251 mg	19.8 g	5.2 g	23.7 g	12.5 g	10.5 g

PRAWN JUNGLE CURRY

SERVES 4

This is one of our favourite dishes—a lighter style curry that is easy to prepare, bursting with freshness and with aromas that will have the whole family running to the table. Unlike most curries, it can be made from start to finish in under 30 minutes and it stores well, making perfect leftovers.

200 ml (7 fl oz) tinned low-fat
  coconut milk, unshaken
3 garlic cloves, thinly sliced
1 thumb-sized piece ginger, grated
4 coriander (cilantro) roots and stems,
  cleaned and thinly sliced (reserve
  the leaves for serving)
¼ teaspoon freshly ground white pepper
1 lemongrass stem, bruised
1 tablespoon fish sauce
1 tablespoon light brown sugar
1 teaspoon ground turmeric
300 ml (10½ fl oz) salt-reduced
  chicken stock
3 kaffir lime leaves
1 red capsicum (pepper), sliced
200 g (7 oz/1 head) broccoli,
  cut into florets
1 handful snow peas (mangetout),
  trimmed
¼ pineapple, cored and diced
40 raw prawns (shrimp), peeled and
  deveined, leaving the tails intact
steamed rice, to serve

Open the coconut milk tin carefully and pour just the creamy white top of the coconut milk into a large frying pan or saucepan placed over high heat. Cook for 1–3 minutes until the coconut milk splits and looks oily. Add the garlic, ginger, coriander, white pepper and lemongrass. Cook, stirring, for 1–2 minutes until fragrant.

Add the fish sauce, brown sugar and turmeric, stir to dissolve, then add the remaining coconut milk, the chicken stock and kaffir lime leaves, and stir to combine. Add the capsicum, broccoli, snow peas and pineapple, and cook until the broccoli and capsicum soften but retains their colour. Add the prawns and cook for a further 2 minutes or until the prawns are cooked through. The prawns will turn white when they are ready. Add a little water at any stage if the curry is lacking moisture.

Serve the prawn jungle curry sprinkled with the reserved coriander leaves and steamed rice.

NUTRITION TIP *This curry is super quick, which means it can easily be jam-packed full of vegetables which will take on the fresh flavours of the curry.*

SUBSTITUTION *In most curries the type of protein is irrelevant. The flavour comes from the sauce or the paste. Prawns make the ideal quick curry but can easily be substituted for chicken, tofu, lentils or chickpeas.*

NUTRITION INFORMATION (PER SERVE)	ENERGY 1167 kJ (279 cal)	PROTEIN 44.0 g	SODIUM 1474 mg	FAT 5.5 g	SAT FAT 3.8 g	CARBOHYDRATE 10.6 g	SUGAR 9.2 g	FIBRE 4.5 g

CAJUN SALMON WITH PEACH SALAD AND DILL YOGHURT

SERVES 4

This dish is so simple, fresh and full of flavour. The crisp, sweet peaches, the crunchy smoked almonds and the toasted Cajun spices give this dish so much flavour with very little effort, and the vibrant colours just scream summer!

130 g (4½ oz/½ cup) low-fat
　Greek-style yoghurt
2 tablespoons wholegrain
　seeded mustard
1 handful dill, chopped
1 tablespoon rice bran oil (or olive oil)
1 tablespoon smoked paprika
1 tablespoon ground cumin
4 x 150 g (5½ oz) salmon fillets, skin on

PEACH SALAD

2 yellow or white peaches, stones
　removed and cut into wedges
large handful rocket (arugula)
1 French shallot, thinly sliced
1 Lebanese (short) cucumber,
　shaved into wide strips using
　a vegetable peeler
2 tablespoons smoked almonds,
　roughly chopped
1 tablespoon olive oil
2 tablespoons white wine vinegar (or
　apple cider vinegar or lemon juice)

Stir together the yoghurt, mustard and dill. Set aside for serving.

Heat the rice bran oil in a non-stick frying pan. Combine the paprika and cumin in a small bowl and coat the flesh side of the salmon with the mixture. Put the salmon in the pan, skin side down, and cook for 2–3 minutes until done to your liking. Turn and repeat with the other side. Remove the salmon from the pan and set aside. Wipe out the pan with paper towel. Add the peach wedges to the pan and cook for 1–2 minutes until golden.

Meanwhile, combine the rocket, shallot and cucumber in a large bowl. Scatter over the almonds and drizzle with the olive oil and white wine vinegar. Combine the peaches with the salad.

Serve the salmon with the peach salad and dill yoghurt.

 NUTRITION TIP *Spices are a great way of adding flavour without using salt, sugar or fat. They also provide a source of nutrition.*

SUBSTITUTION *Try plums or nectarines instead of peaches. If you want to prepare this dish in another season, pears or apples also work well.*
Substitute the salmon for a piece of thick white fish, chicken tenderloins or a pork cutlet. Just remember you will need to adjust the cooking time depending on the meat you choose.

NUTRITION INFORMATION (PER SERVE)	ENERGY	PROTEIN	SODIUM	FAT	SAT FAT	CARBOHYDRATE	SUGAR	FIBRE
	2312 kJ (552 cal)	47.8 g	288 mg	32.1 g	7.5 g	15.8 g	13.2 g	4.7 g

QUICK · EASY · HEALTHY ·

61

GRILLED LAMB WITH OLIVE TAPENADE AND TOMATO SALAD

SERVES 4

A premium cut of lean meat such as lamb backstrap is best prepared quickly to ensure it remains moist and tender. This dish is quick but still packs a flavour punch from the olive tapenade, generous spices, fresh herbs and balsamic dressing. A full-flavoured dinner in only minutes!

2 teaspoons ground cumin
2 teaspoons smoked paprika
2 x 200 g (7 oz) lamb backstraps
1 tablespoons rice bran oil (or olive oil)
120 g (4½ oz/¾ cup) pitted
   kalamata olives
2 garlic cloves, crushed or
   finely chopped
1 tablespoon capers, rinsed
1 tablespoon balsamic vinegar
60 ml (2 fl oz/¼ cup) extra virgin olive oil

TOMATO SALAD
500 g (1 lb 2 oz) tomatoes (preferably
   a mix of small and large)
3 handfuls basil, leaves picked
1 tablespoon capers, rinsed
1 French shallot, thinly sliced
2 tablespoons olive oil
2 tablespoons balsamic vinegar

Stir the cumin and paprika together in a small bowl. Rub the mixture into both sides of the lamb.

Heat a chargrill pan or barbecue to high heat. Brush the lamb with rice bran oil and cook on one side for 3–4 minutes or until golden brown. Turn over and continue to fry until cooked to your liking. Remove the lamb and rest, lightly covered, on a plate.

Meanwhile, blend the olives, garlic, capers and balsamic vinegar in a food processor until finely chopped. Add the olive oil, then blitz again briefly until just combined.

Slice the tomatoes into different shapes and sizes. Combine in a bowl with the basil leaves, capers, French shallot, olive oil and balsamic vinegar. Season with a little salt and pepper.

Slice the lamb into thick pieces and serve with the tomato salad and olive tapenade.

 NUTRITION TIP *Preparing your own dips and spreads, such as this olive tapenade, is super simple and you know what goes into them. You can also use extra virgin olive oil for a delicious flavour and quality nutrition.*

SUBSTITUTION *If you don't have ground cumin or smoked paprika, try ground coriander or dried herbs such as oregano and thyme.*

NUTRITION INFORMATION (PER SERVE)	ENERGY 1991 kJ (476 cal)	PROTEIN 24.5 g	SODIUM 733 mg	FAT 38.3 g	SAT FAT 6.9 g	CARBOHYDRATE 6.5 g	SUGAR 4.5 g	FIBRE 4.2 g

CHILLI-RUBBED CHICKEN WITH AVOCADO, CORN AND LIME SALAD

SERVES 4

There is quick, and then there is this dish! You should have this delicious, balanced meal on the table in under 20 minutes, and you won't have a kitchen full of dishes at the end either!

AVOCADO, CORN AND LIME SALAD
1 avocado, diced
400 g (14 oz) tinned kidney beans, rinsed and drained
3 spring onions (scallions), thinly sliced
juice of 2 limes
1 tablespoon olive oil
4 corn cobs, kernels removed

¼ teaspoon chilli powder
2 tablespoons smoked paprika
8 chicken tenderloins (about 450 g/1 lb)
1 tablespoon olive oil

Combine the avocado, kidney beans, spring onion, lime juice and olive oil in a large bowl. Set aside.

Combine the chilli powder and paprika in a small bowl then use the mixture to coat the chicken. Heat a frying pan over high heat and add the oil. Add the chicken and cook for 2–3 minutes on each side until just cooked. Remove the chicken from the pan and set aside.

Add the corn to the pan and cook for 1–2 minutes, stirring, until the corn is bright yellow and tender. Stir the corn through the avocado and lime salad and serve with the chicken.

 NUTRITION TIP *Beans are a great source of fibre, protein and low-GI carbohydrate. They keep us energised and full for longer.*

SUBSTITUTION *Not a fan of kidney beans? Try chickpeas, lentils or even tofu fried in the leftover spices from the chicken.*

NUTRITION INFORMATION (PER SERVE)	ENERGY 2089 kJ (499 cal)	PROTEIN 35.9 g	SODIUM 247 mg	FAT 25.0 g	SAT FAT 5.0 g	CARBOHYDRATE 26.0 g	SUGAR 7.4 g	FIBRE 13.9 g

PEACH MELBA AND YOGHURT ETON MESS

SERVES 4

Using yoghurt instead of cream takes this dish from a rich sweet pavlova to a more refreshing summer dessert. Usually meringue-based dishes take a while to cook. These small meringues cook in no time, making this a great last-minute sweet.

1 egg white
2 tablespoons caster (superfine) sugar
170 ml (5½ fl oz/⅔ cup) thickened (whipping) cream
130 g (4½ oz/½ cup) low-fat Greek-style yoghurt
2 tablespoons icing (confectioners') sugar
2 teaspoons vanilla bean paste (or vanilla extract)
70 g (2½ oz) raspberries (or frozen raspberries, defrosted), plus 125 g (4½ oz/1 cup) extra to serve
2 yellow peaches, cut into wedges, to serve
2 tablespoons toasted flaked almonds, to serve

Preheat the oven to 100°C (200°F/Gas ½). Line a baking tray with baking paper.

Place the egg white in a large bowl. Use electric beaters or a whisk to whip the egg to soft peaks, then slowly add the caster sugar, whisking all the time, until stiff and glossy. Using a piping (icing) bag or snipped snap-lock bag, pipe the meringue into 1 cm (½ inch) dots onto the prepared tray. Transfer to the oven and bake for 12–14 minutes or until the meringues crisp up a little. Remove from the oven and leave to cool.

Meanwhile, combine the cream, yoghurt, icing sugar and vanilla bean paste, and whip to soft peaks. Mash the raspberries to a thick sauce consistency with a fork.

Combine the meringue with the cream and yoghurt mixture. Fold through the raspberry sauce. Don't overmix, to ensure you get swirls of raspberry sauce going through the white cream. Divide among four dessert glasses, top with the peach slices, fresh raspberries and almonds and serve.

 NUTRITION TIP *We've substituted some of the cream for Greek-style yoghurt which reduces the fat content and adds a lovely fresh acidity.*

SUBSTITUTION *Blueberries, blackberries, apricots, plums or any summer fruit will work in this dish.*

NUTRITION INFORMATION (PER SERVE)	ENERGY 1340 kJ (320 cal)	PROTEIN 6.2 g	SODIUM 58 mg	FAT 18.8 g	SAT FAT 10.4 g	CARBOHYDRATE 27.8 g	SUGAR 27.3 g	FIBRE 5.1 g

FROZEN YOGHURT WITH TOASTED NUTS AND SEEDS

SERVES 4

This is a great light summer dessert. Make a large batch of frozen yoghurt and save it for those times when you have a craving for something sweet. The toasted nut and seed mix adds a contrasting texture to the frozen yoghurt, and the cranberries and blueberries provide a natural sweetness.

400 g (14 oz) low-fat
   Greek-style yoghurt
1 tablespoon honey
30 g (1½ oz/¼ cup) pistachio nuts,
   broken up slightly
40 g (1½ oz/¼ cup) almonds,
   roughly chopped
40 g (1½ oz/¼ cup) pepitas
   (pumpkin seeds)
15 g (½ oz/¼ cup) flaked or
   shredded coconut
1 teaspoon ground cinnamon
1 tablespoon light brown sugar
40 g (1½ oz/¼ cup) dried cranberries
125 g (4½ oz) blueberries, to serve

To make the frozen yoghurt, combine the yoghurt and honey in a bowl. Transfer to a freezer-safe container and freeze for 2–3 hours until firm.

Preheat the oven to 180°C (350°F/Gas 4).

Combine the pistachios, almonds, pepitas, coconut, cinnamon and sugar in a bowl and mix until the cinnamon is well distributed. Place the mixture onto a baking tray, transfer to the oven and toast for 8–12 minutes until the mixture is golden and smells delicious.

Remove the mixture from the oven, tip into a bowl or container and stir through the cranberries. Leave to cool for a few minutes. Remove the yoghurt from the freezer and use a fork to scrape into a fine snow consistency. Divide among four dessert glasses or tumblers, top with the toasted mixture and the blueberries, and serve.

 NUTRITION TIP *This dish is full of polyunsaturated and mono-unsaturated fats from the nuts and seeds. Although these fats are healthy, they are still energy-dense. If you are watching your energy intake, go easy on the nuts.*

SUBSTITUTION *If you don't have time for frozen yoghurt, try topping some ricotta and fresh fruit with the nut and seed mix.*

NUTRITION INFORMATION (PER SERVE)	ENERGY	PROTEIN	SODIUM	FAT	SAT FAT	CARBOHYDRATE	SUGAR	FIBRE
	1286 kJ (307 cal)	12.4 g	88 mg	15.8 g	4.2 g	27.2 g	25.7 g	3.8 g

BRIOCHE WITH RICOTTA, ROASTED PEACHES AND HONEY SYRUP

SERVES 4

As far as sweets go, they don't get much easier (or healthier!) than this summer treat. The creaminess from the ricotta, topped with fresh fruit, then a drizzle of sweet and sour syrup makes this brioche a perfect summer dessert or weekend brunch.

2 yellow peaches, quartered
4 slices brioche
250 g (9 oz) low-fat ricotta cheese
2 teaspoons rosewater, to taste
2 tablespoons toasted pecans,
   roughly chopped

HONEY SYRUP
1 lemon
50 g (1¾ oz) honey
1 cinnamon stick (or 1 teaspoon
   ground cinnamon)
1 teaspoon vanilla bean paste
   (or vanilla extract)
5 thyme sprigs

Preheat the oven to 200°C (400°F/Gas 6). Line a baking tray with baking paper.

Place the peaches on the prepared tray, cut side up, and transfer to the oven. Cook for 15–20 minutes or until tender but not completely falling apart. Alternatively, grill the fruits on a barbecue grill plate or chargrill pan over high heat until caramelised and slightly charred.

Meanwhile, to make the honey syrup, peel the zest from the lemon and place in a small saucepan. Squeeze in the juice, then add 2 tablespoons of water and the remaining ingredients, and gently bring to a simmer, stirring until the sugar has dissolved. Leave to cool slightly and for the flavours to infuse for 5 minutes. Strain.

Toast the brioche in a hot dry frying pan for 1 minute on each side or until golden, then remove from the pan.

Stir together the ricotta and rosewater. Divide the brioche among four serving plates, spoon over the ricotta and rosewater, top with the caramelised peaches, honey syrup and chopped pecans and serve.

 NUTRITION TIP *With 28 g of carbohydrate and 11 g of protein this is a great recovery snack post exercise.*

SUBSTITUTION *If you can't find brioche, fruit bread is a good replacement.*

NUTRITION INFORMATION (PER SERVE)	ENERGY	PROTEIN	SODIUM	FAT	SAT FAT	CARBOHYDRATE	SUGAR	FIBRE
	1158 kJ (277 cal)	11.4 g	197 mg	12.4 g	5.8 g	28.1 g	20.1 g	3.5 g

RASPBERRY YOGHURT PARFAIT WITH BLUEBERRIES AND PEACHES

SERVES 8

Most parfaits are made with meringue and cream, however, this recipe uses yoghurt as a healthier alternative. Aside from the freezing time this is a super quick dessert—whack it in the freezer at night and enjoy it around the pool the next day!

260 g (9¼ oz/1 cup) low-fat Greek-style yoghurt
2 teaspoons vanilla bean paste (or vanilla extract)
finely grated zest of 1 lemon
3 egg whites
55 g (2 oz/¼ cup) caster (superfine) sugar
125 g (4½ oz) frozen raspberries
30 g (1 oz/¼ cup) pistachio nuts, roughly chopped
4 peaches, sliced into wedges, to serve
125 g (4½ oz) blueberries, to serve

Line a 22 x 12 cm (8½ x 4½ inch) loaf (bar) tin with plastic wrap. Stir together the yoghurt, vanilla bean paste and lemon zest.

Place the egg whites in a large bowl. Use electric beaters or a whisk to whip the eggs to soft peaks, then slowly add the sugar, whisking all the time, until a stiff, shiny meringue is reached.

Use a whisk to fold the egg white mixture and yoghurt mixture together. Carefully fold through the raspberries and pistachios. Try not to overmix as the raspberries will bleed and turn the parfait pink.

Spoon the parfait mixture into the loaf tin and smooth with a spatula or knife. Freeze for 4 hours or overnight until firm.

Turn the parfait out, remove the plastic wrap and slice into 8 pieces. Divide the parfait slices among serving plates. Serve with the peach wedges and blueberries.

 NUTRITION TIP *For an added nutrition boost, add your favourite seeds or nuts along with the pistachios.*

SUBSTITUTION *If you don't have any vanilla bean paste, try using vanilla-flavoured yoghurt or add 2 teaspoons of honey to natural yoghurt.*

NUTRITION INFORMATION (PER SERVE)	ENERGY	PROTEIN	SODIUM	FAT	SAT FAT	CARBOHYDRATE	SUGAR	FIBRE
	538 kJ (128 cal)	5.3 g	49 mg	2.4 g	0.3 g	18.6 g	18.1 g	3.3 g

LEMON CUSTARD, GRANITA AND SUMMER FRUIT

SERVES 4

We love a good custard and, by 'we', we mean Themis. The addition of lemon zest to this dessert and the lemon granita takes the dish from a cup of sweet custard to a balanced dessert.

2 white nectarines, cut into wedges
1 large handful cherries, pitted
    and halved

LEMON GRANITA
55 g (2 oz/¼ cup) caster
    (superfine) sugar
zest and juice of 2 lemons

LEMON CUSTARD
375 ml (13 fl oz/1½ cups) low-fat milk
1 tablespoon honey
finely grated zest of 2 lemons
1 teaspoon vanilla bean paste
3 egg yolks
1 tablespoon cornflour (cornstarch)

Preheat the oven to 190°C (375°F/Gas 5).

To make the lemon granita, combine the sugar, lemon zest and 170 ml (5½ fl oz/⅔ cup) of water in a saucepan. Place over medium–high heat and cook for 2–3 minutes, stirring occasionally, until the sugar has dissolved. Remove from the heat and stir in the lemon juice. Remove any large chunks of lemon zest. Transfer to a shallow freezer-safe tray or container and freeze for 2–4 hours until firm.

To make the lemon custard, place the milk, honey, lemon zest and vanilla bean paste in a small saucepan. Bring the milk mixture to the boil, then remove from the heat.

Meanwhile, whisk together the egg yolks and cornflour in a bowl. Pour the hot milk into the bowl and whisk to combine. Pour the mixture back into the saucepan and cook, whisking, until the custard boils and thickens. Transfer to a container or bowl and leave to cool until ready to serve.

To serve, spoon the lemon custard into four dessert glasses and top with the nectarine wedges and cherries. Scrape the granita into fine crystals using a fork (or use a food processor), then spoon over the top and serve.

NUTRITION TIP *Making your own custard allows you to control how much sugar is used and the fat content of the milk.*

SUBSTITUTION *If you don't have lemons, the zest of any citrus can be used in the custard, while the juice can be used in the granita.*

NUTRITION INFORMATION (PER SERVE)	ENERGY	PROTEIN	SODIUM	FAT	SAT FAT	CARBOHYDRATE	SUGAR	FIBRE
	888 kJ (212 cal)	6.6 g	53 mg	3.3 g	1.1 g	37.8 g	34.8 g	2.5 g

QUINOA, MANGO AND RASPBERRY PUDDING

SERVES 4

This dish is perfect for those who desire a more subtly sweet dish. Smooth in consistency, naturally sweet and nutty in flavour, it makes a great dessert or the perfect snack. Enjoy hot or cold.

100 g (3½ oz/½ cup) quinoa
2 tablespoons chia seeds
400 ml (14 fl oz) tinned low-fat coconut milk
2 teaspoons vanilla bean paste (or vanilla extract)
2 tablespoons honey
1 mango, diced
250 g (9 oz/2 cups) raspberries (or blackberries), halved
30 g (1 oz/¼ cup) pistachio nuts, toasted and roughly chopped

Combine the quinoa, chia seeds, coconut milk, vanilla bean paste and 125 ml (4 fl oz/½ cup) of water in a saucepan. Bring to a gentle simmer over medium–high heat, then reduce the heat and cook for 12–18 minutes until the quinoa is tender and the mixture has thickened.

Remove the quinoa from the heat and stir through the honey. Spoon onto four dessert plates. Top each with mango, raspberries and pistachios and serve.

 NUTRITION TIP *This dessert, unlike most, offers a large amount of quality nutrition from the quinoa, chia seeds, fruit and nuts. It is also gluten-free. Increase the protein content by using cow's milk.*

SUBSTITUTION *If you're out of quinoa, try using arborio rice or sago. Or try using oats and cut back on the vanilla bean paste and honey for a delicious breakfast. Just remember though, oats contain gluten, so this substitution is not appropriate for individuals with coeliac disease.*

NUTRITION INFORMATION (PER SERVE)	ENERGY 1453 kJ (347 cal)	PROTEIN 7.4 g	SODIUM 26 mg	FAT 15.6 g	SAT FAT 7.4 g	CARBOHYDRATE 41.0 g	SUGAR 25.0 g	FIBRE 5.7 g

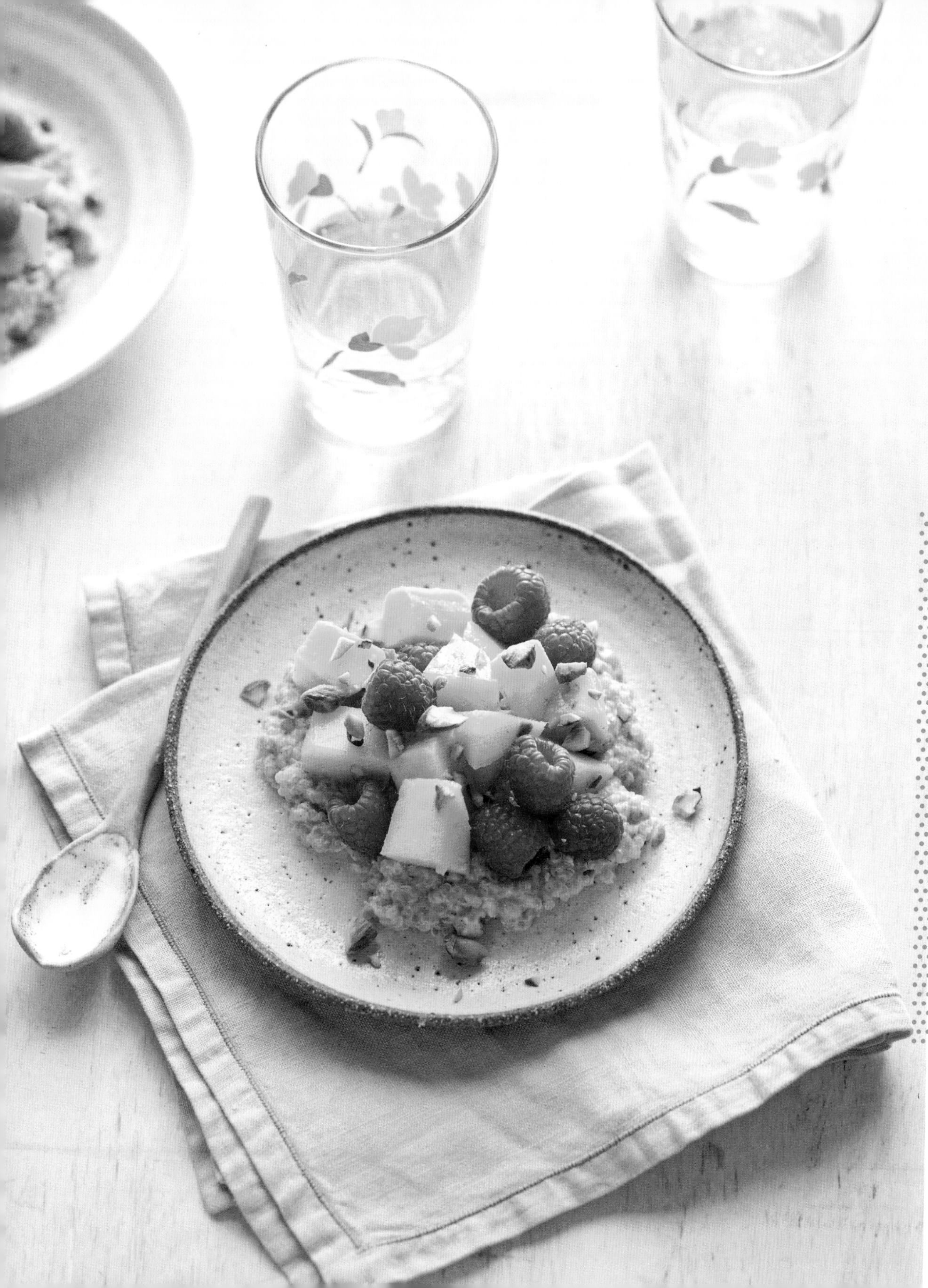

AUTUMN

EARTHY. WARMING. HEARTY.

As the temperature begins to cool, we begin to shift from alfresco dining to the comfort of indoors, and we we cover the barbecue to allow the cobwebs to build again for another year.

We start to move from light, fresh, summer dishes and look towards slightly richer, warming meals. It's time to turn on the oven and welcome roasted vegetables into our dinners, such as Roast cauliflower and pumpkin with tahini yoghurt (page 85), and heartier desserts like our Orange and honey ricotta ten-minute brûlée (page 114). A few more satisfying legumes and whole grains, such as quinoa and freekeh, begin to appear, which complement the earthy tones of autumn vegetables, such as mushrooms and beetroot (beets).

AUTUMN SHOPPING LIST

As the last of the summer fruits empty our shelves sweet, antioxidant-rich pomegranates and figs take their place. Figs are a good source of fibre and their antioxidant content actually increases as they ripen. Look for plump, juicy figs, but not too soft. Pomegranates are nutrition powerhouses. Packed full of vitamins, particularly C, K and folate, they also provide a very rich source of fibre and antioxidants. Look for pomegranates that have firm skins, not ones that look old and leathery.

When it comes to autumn vegetables, it's all about the leafy greens: kale, spinach, silverbeet and Asian greens—and don't forget the leaves of vegetables such as beetroot and celery. Leafy greens are a good source of vitamins such as folate and they bulk out a meal without adding many kilojoules (calories). Fill up on these!

VEGETABLES

- ASIAN GREENS
- ASPARAGUS
- BEAN SPROUTS
- BEANS
- BEETROOT
  (BEETS)
- BOK CHOY
- BROCCOLI
- BRUSSELS
  SPROUTS
- CABBAGE
- CAPSICUMS
  (PEPPER)
- CARROTS
- CAULIFLOWER
- CELERIAC
- CELERY
- CHESTNUTS
- CHOKOS
- CUCUMBERS
- EGGPLANT
  (AUBERGINES)
- FENNEL
- FRENCH
  SHALLOTS
- GINGER
- KALE
- LEEKS
- LETTUCE
- MUSHROOMS
- OKRA
- ONIONS
- PARSNIPS
- POTATOES
- PUMPKIN
  (WINTER SQUASH)
- RHUBARB
- SILVERBEET
  (SWISS CHARD)
- SNOW PEAS
  (MANGETOUT)
- SPINACH
- SPRING ONIONS
  (SCALLIONS)
- SWEET POTATO
- SWEETCORN
- TOMATOES
- TURNIPS
- WITLOF
- ZUCCHINI
  (COURGETTES)

FRUIT

- APPLES
- AVOCADOS
- BANANAS
- CUSTARD APPLES
- DATES
- FIGS
- GRAPES
- GUAVA
- IMPERIAL
  MANDARINS
- KIWI FRUIT
- LEMONS
- LIMES
- MANGOSTEENS
- NASHI PEARS
- NAVEL ORANGES
- NECTARINES
- PAPAYA
- PASSIONFRUIT
- PEACHES
- PEARS
- PERSIMMONS
- PLUMS
- POMEGRANATES
- QUINCES
- RHUBARB
- TAMARILLO
- VALENCIA
  ORANGES
- WATERMELON

BEETROOT-CURED SALMON WITH LEMON RICOTTA ON RYE

Visually stunning, yet so simple, this dish makes a great breakfast, brunch or light lunch. The earthy tones of the beetroot and the fresh lemon and dill marry perfectly with the cured salmon.

BEETROOT-CURED SALMON
1 beetroot (beet), coarsely grated
1 handful dill, roughly chopped
110 g (3¾ oz/½ cup) caster
 (superfine) sugar
105 g (3½ oz/⅓ cup) rock salt
2 x 200 g (7 oz) skinless salmon fillets

250 g (9 oz) low-fat ricotta cheese
zest of 1 lemon
4 thick slices rye bread, toasted,
 to serve
1 handful dill, roughly chopped

To make the beetroot-cured salmon, combine the beetroot, dill, sugar and salt in a bowl. Place a large piece of plastic wrap—long enough to enclose the salmon—on a tray.

Spread half the beetroot mixture over the plastic wrap, top with the salmon, side by side, and pack around the remaining beetroot mixture so the fillets are completely enclosed. Wrap the fish tightly in the plastic wrap and refrigerate for 8–10 hours, turning the fish over, re-covering with the beetroot mixture and rewrapping halfway through the curing process.

Unwrap the salmon and use paper towel to wipe off the beetroot mixture. Thinly slice the salmon using a long, sharp knife. Stir together the ricotta and lemon zest, then spread over the toasted rye. Pile over the salmon slices and top with fresh dill to serve.

NUTRITION TIP *Don't worry about the amount of sugar and salt in the cure, it's only used during the preparation, and isn't eaten. Add some vegetables to this recipe to create a balanced meal. Try grilled mushrooms, roasted capsicums (peppers) or roasted tomatoes.*

SUBSTITUTION *Try tuna or kingfish if salmon is hard to find. If dill is not available try thyme or parsley.*

NUTRITION INFORMATION (PER SERVE)	ENERGY	PROTEIN	SODIUM	FAT	SAT FAT	CARBOHYDRATE	SUGAR	FIBRE
	1754 kJ (419 cal)	38.0 g	321 mg	18.6 g	6.7 g	23.2 g	4.6 g	3.3 g

ROAST CAULIFLOWER AND PUMPKIN WITH TAHINI YOGHURT

SERVES 4

This dish is a great example of how delicious vegetables can be if you put a little effort in and use your imagination. The spices add deep rich flavour and the yoghurt dressing provides a burst of freshness.

1 teaspoon ground turmeric

1 teaspoon smoked paprika

1 tablespoon olive oil, plus ½ tablespoon extra

300 g (10½ oz/¼ head) cauliflower, cut into 2 cm (1 inch) florets

200 g (7 oz/about ¼) butternut pumpkin (squash), peeled and cut into 1.5 cm (⅝ inch) cubes

400 g (14 oz) tinned chickpeas, rinsed and drained

2 tablespoons sesame seeds

2 tablespoons coriander seeds

1 tablespoon cumin seeds

190 g (6¾ oz/⅔ cup) low-fat Greek-style yoghurt

1 tablespoon tahini

1 tablespoon wholegrain mustard

zest and juice of 1 lemon

1 small zucchini (courgette), shaved into thin strips using a vegetable peeler

2 tablespoons roasted almonds, roughly chopped

2 tablespoons currants

2 handfuls coriander (cilantro), leaves picked and roughly chopped

Preheat the oven to 200°C (400°F/Gas 6).

Combine the turmeric, paprika and olive oil in a large bowl, then toss through the cauliflower and pumpkin. Transfer onto a baking tray, arrange in a single layer, and bake for 30–35 minutes until the tips are golden brown and the cauliflower and pumpkin have softened. Add the chickpeas for the final 10 minutes of cooking, to heat through.

Meanwhile, heat a frying pan over medium–high heat. Add the sesame seeds, coriander seeds and cumin seeds. Toast for 1–2 minutes until lightly golden and fragrant. Tip into a small food processor, or use a mortar and pestle, and crush until coarsely ground.

Put the yoghurt, tahini, mustard and lemon zest in a small bowl and stir to combine.

Remove the cauliflower, pumpkin and chickpeas from the oven and transfer into a large bowl. Toss through the remaining 2 teaspoons of olive oil, the lemon juice, zucchini, almonds and currants. Serve with the tahini yoghurt topped with the ground spices and chopped coriander.

 NUTRITION TIP *Nuts, seeds and legumes provide valuable sources of protein and healthy fats in vegetarian meals.*

SUBSTITUTION *If no meal is complete for you without a protein, try serving this salad with oven baked chicken breast marinated in olive oil, thyme and lemon zest.*

NUTRITION INFORMATION (PER SERVE)	ENERGY 1624 kJ (388 cal)	PROTEIN 13.8 g	SODIUM 303 mg	FAT 21.3 g	SAT FAT 4.0 g	CARBOHYDRATE 30.0 g	SUGAR 17.0 g	FIBRE 10.7 g

MUSHROOM AND SPINACH FRITTATA WITH RADICCHIO SALAD

SERVES 4

People often ask us if there is actually a difference between types of mushrooms. Well, yes, there is—they all differ in taste and texture. Find the mushrooms that you love the most or, if you're like us, mix them together!

1½ tablespoons olive oil
300 g (10½ oz) mixed mushrooms, sliced
3 garlic cloves, crushed or finely chopped
8 thyme sprigs, leaves picked
½ teaspoon chilli flakes (optional)
2 handfuls baby spinach
8 eggs
80 ml (2½ fl oz/⅓ cup) low-fat milk
30 g (1 oz) parmesan cheese, finely grated

RADICCHIO SALAD
1 radicchio, leaves separated
1 pear, thinly sliced
1 zucchini (courgette), shaved into thin strips
2 tablespoons balsamic vinegar
1 tablespoon olive oil

Preheat the oven to 180°C (350°F/Gas 4). Grease and line a 20 cm (8 inch) springform cake tin.

Heat the olive oil in a large frying pan over high heat. Add half the mushrooms and cook for 1–2 minutes on each side until browned. Remove from the pan, and repeat with the remaining mushrooms. Return all the mushrooms to the pan with the garlic, thyme and chilli flakes, if using. Cook, stirring for a minute or until the garlic softens, then stir through the spinach until just wilted. Transfer the mushroom mixture to the prepared cake tin and arrange to form an even layer.

Whisk together the eggs, milk and parmesan, then pour over the mushroom mixture. Bake the frittata for 18–25 minutes until golden brown and puffy.

Meanwhile, combine the radicchio, pear, zucchini, balsamic vinegar and olive oil in a large bowl.

Remove the frittata from the oven and set aside to cool for 5–10 minutes, then remove from the tin and cut into wedges. Serve with the radicchio salad.

 NUTRITION TIP *Along with the sun, mushrooms are a good source of vitamin D.*

SUBSTITUTION *If you can't find fresh thyme, use rosemary. If you are short on mushrooms, include some pan-fried diced zucchini or pumpkin (winter squash) in the mixture.*

NUTRITION INFORMATION (PER SERVE)	ENERGY	PROTEIN	SODIUM	FAT	SAT FAT	CARBOHYDRATE	SUGAR	FIBRE
	998 kJ (238 cal)	16.9 g	226 mg	17.1 g	5.2 g	3.4 g	1.9 g	2.5 g

LAMB KOFTA WITH HARISSA

SERVES 4

This dish is great for entertaining or for those who like to be organised and plan ahead. You can roll the kofta a few hours before cooking, or even pre-cook and reheat them when you are ready to go.

500 g (1 lb 2 oz) minced (ground) lamb
2 teaspoons cumin seeds
2 teaspoons fennel seeds
1 tablespoon rice bran oil (or olive oil)
1 pomegranate
2 large handfuls rocket (arugula)
2 zucchini (courgettes), shaved into
    strips using a vegetable peeler
2 tablespoons pistachio nuts,
    roughly chopped
1 handful mint, leaves picked
1 tablespoon olive oil
juice of 1 lemon
flat bread, to serve

HARISSA
200 g (7 oz) roasted capsicum
    (pepper) pieces
1 long red chilli, seeded
    (you don't want much heat)
2 teaspoons ground cumin
juice of 1 lemon

Eggplant and pomegranate salad
    (see page 94), to serve (optional)

To make the harissa, combine the roasted capsicum pieces, chilli, cumin and lemon juice in a small food processor. Blend until smooth.

Combine the lamb, cumin seeds and fennel seeds in a bowl. Roll into 2.5 cm (1 inch) balls, to make 12 balls.

Heat the rice bran oil in a non-stick frying pan over high heat. Add the kofta balls and cook, turning occasionally, for 3–4 minutes until golden brown all over and just cooked.

Cut the pomegranate in half. Holding the cut side facing down in the palm of your hand, use a wooden spoon to repeatedly knock the pomegranate until the seeds fall out. Put all the seeds in a large bowl and add the rocket, zucchini, pistachios, half the mint leaves, the olive oil and lemon juice. Combine.

Spread the harissa onto a big serving board and top with the kofta. Pile the pomegranate salad next to it, top with the remaining mint leaves and serve with flat bread.

 NUTRITION TIP *Where possible choose a lean mince as it is lower in saturated fat, which is a key contributor to heart disease.*

SUBSTITUTION *Instead of harissa, try pesto or natural yoghurt with lemon zest and mint.*

NUTRITION INFORMATION (PER SERVE)	ENERGY 2032 kJ (485 cal)	PROTEIN 32.7 g	SODIUM 170 mg	FAT 28.2 g	SAT FAT 8.3 g	CARBOHYDRATE 21.5 g	SUGAR 13.2 g	FIBRE 8.2 g

ROAST EGGPLANT WITH PISTACHIO DUKKAH

We have a simple rule when it comes to cooking eggplant. When you think it's done, cook it some more! Don't let its soft texture fool you, this vegetable is durable and can handle the heat. Thinly sliced and pan-fried or oven-roasted it benefits from plenty of high heat and time.

2 small–medium eggplants (aubergines), halved lengthways, flesh scored in a criss-cross pattern
1½ tablespoons olive oil
30 g (1 oz) feta cheese, crumbled (optional)
seeds from 1 pomegranate (see method page 87)
2 tablespoons pomegranate molasses, to serve
1 handful mint, leaves picked, to serve (optional)

PISTACHIO DUKKAH
2 tablespoons pistachio nuts
2 tablespoons sesame seeds
2 tablespoons coriander seeds
1½ teaspoons fennel seeds
2 teaspoons cumin seeds
1 teaspoon smoked paprika (optional)

Preheat the oven to 180°C (350°F/Gas 4).

Lay the eggplants cut sides up on a baking tray. Drizzle the eggplant flesh with the olive oil. Transfer to the oven and roast for 35–45 minutes until softened and golden.

To make the pistachio dukkah, heat a frying pan over medium–high heat. Add the pistachios, sesame seeds, coriander seeds, fennel seeds and cumin seeds, and toast for 1–2 minutes until lightly golden and fragrant. Add the paprika, if using, then tip into a small food processor, or use a mortar and pestle, and crush until coarsely ground.

Remove the eggplant from the oven and divide among four plates. Spoon some dukkah over each. Top with feta, if using. Scatter over the pomegranate seeds, drizzle with the pomegranate molasses, scatter over the mint leaves, if using, and serve.

 NUTRITION TIP *Eggplant acts like a sponge and sucks up oil. If you want to limit your oil consumption, oven-roasting is a better option rather than pan-frying.*

SUBSTITUTION *You can use any crumbly fresh cheese instead of feta. Kalamata olives are also a good substitute as they provide a similar fresh, salty flavour.*
You could also substitute pomegranates for dried cranberries at another time of year.

NUTRITION INFORMATION (PER SERVE)	ENERGY	PROTEIN	SODIUM	FAT	SAT FAT	CARBOHYDRATE	SUGAR	FIBRE
	1092 kJ (261 cal)	6.6 g	103 mg	15.4 g	3.0 g	19.8 g	19.2 g	8.6 g

THAI SWEET POTATO AND BEEF SALAD

SERVES 4

This salad is big, bright and full of texture. The roasted sweet potato, while not overly traditional in Thai cuisine, is a satisfying addition; the green beans, cashews and bean sprouts provide important crunch; and the mint and coriander provide the fresh fragrant tones that make Thai food so popular.

400 g (14 oz) sweet potato, cut into 1.5–2 cm (⅝–¾ inch) cubes
1 tablespoon olive oil
2 teaspoons ground cumin
1 tablespoon rice bran oil (or olive oil)
2 x 200 g (7 oz) beef porterhouse steaks
1 large handful green beans, topped and tailed
40 g (1½ oz/¼ cup) roasted unsalted cashew nuts
115 g (4 oz/1 cup) bean sprouts
3 spring onions (scallions), thinly sliced
3 handfuls mint, leaves picked

THAI DRESSING
1 tablespoon fish sauce
juice of 1 lemon
1½ tablespoons light brown sugar
3 handfuls coriander (cilantro), leaves picked and reserved for the salad, stems thinly sliced
1 long red chilli, seeded and thinly sliced

Preheat the oven to 200°C (400°F/Gas 6).

Combine the sweet potato, olive oil and cumin in a bowl. Transfer onto a baking tray, arrange in a single layer, and roast for 20–25 minutes until golden and tender.

To make the Thai dressing, combine the fish sauce, lemon juice, sugar, coriander stems and chilli in a small bowl and stir until the sugar has dissolved. Taste the dressing and adjust if necessary. Set aside.

Heat the rice bran oil in a frying pan over high heat. Put the steaks in the pan and cook for 3–4 minutes per side until cooked to your liking. Remove to a board to rest for about half the time it was cooked.

Meanwhile, add the beans to the pan and cook for 2–3 minutes until slightly charred and just tender. Add a splash of water if needed to assist cooking.

Combine the cashews, bean sprouts, spring onion, mint leaves and reserved coriander leaves with the dressing in a large bowl. Gently mix through the sweet potato and green beans. Thinly slice the beef, add to the salad and serve immediately.

 NUTRITION TIP *Sweet potato is a great low-GI carbohydrate.*

SUBSTITUTION *You can swap the steak for any type of meat—chicken, pork or even duck.*

NUTRITION INFORMATION (PER SERVE)	ENERGY 1757 kJ (420 cal)	PROTEIN 31.8 g	SODIUM 567 mg	FAT 17.7 g	SAT FAT 3.9 g	CARBOHYDRATE 30.2 g	SUGAR 15.8 g	FIBRE 7.1 g

CAMBODIAN BEEF, PUMPKIN AND COCONUT STIR-FRY

SERVES 4

This dish packs heaps of flavours into one wok. The key to the perfect stir-fry is to be well prepared, use a blistering high heat and cook every component for a short time. This will help the vegetables to retain their appealing colours and textures.

1 tablespoon rice bran oil (or olive oil)
200 g (7 oz) beef sirloin steaks
  (or porterhouse or fillet),
  cut into thin strips
400 g (14 oz/about ½) butternut
  pumpkin (squash), cut into 1 cm
  (½ inch) cubes
3 garlic cloves, thinly sliced
1 long red chilli, thinly sliced
1 lemongrass stem, bruised
2 handfuls coriander (cilantro),
  leaves picked, stems thinly sliced
25 g (1 oz) roasted unsalted cashew
  nuts, roughly chopped
1 teaspoon ground turmeric
4 spring onions (scallions), thinly sliced
1 large handful green beans, topped
  and tailed
3 bok choy (pak choy), quartered
2 tablespoons fish sauce
1 tablespoon light brown sugar
200 ml (7 fl oz) tinned low-fat
  coconut milk
steamed brown rice, to serve

Heat a wok or large frying pan over high heat. Add the rice bran oil, then the beef. Cook, stirring occasionally, for 30 seconds or until lightly browned. Remove the beef from the wok and set aside. Add the pumpkin, garlic, chilli, lemongrass and coriander stems. Cook for 3–4 minutes. Stir in the cashews and turmeric and cook for 1–2 minutes, until fragrant and starting to change colour, then add half the spring onion, the green beans and bok choy. Give the ingredients in the wok a good toss around, then stir in the fish sauce, sugar and coconut milk, and cook for 1–2 minutes until the pumpkin softens. Add the beef and warm through. Discard the lemongrass.

Serve the Cambodian beef stir-fry in the middle of the table with steamed brown rice topped with the remaining spring onion and the coriander leaves.

NUTRITION TIP *This dish makes great leftovers! Avoid takeaway foods at the office—take this to work and squeeze a few extra vegetables in for a healthy lunch.*

SUBSTITUTION *If you don't have fish sauce, or if you have a friend who's allergic to seafood, use light soy sauce. They both contribute salt to the dish and balance the sweetness of the sugar.*

NUTRITION INFORMATION (PER SERVE)	ENERGY	PROTEIN	SODIUM	FAT	SAT FAT	CARBOHYDRATE	SUGAR	FIBRE
	1403 kJ (335 cal)	27.0 g	1065 mg	16.3 g	6.2 g	16.6 g	12.7 g	7.7 g

SPICED FISH WITH EGGPLANT AND POMEGRANATE SALAD

SERVES 4

Pomegranates have a short season so you need to use them while you can. They are super versatile and feature in many of our sweet and savoury dishes. Just be careful that they don't stain your kitchen a beautiful shade of pink!

1 tablespoon ground cumin
1 tablespoon ground coriander
4 x 120 g (4¼ oz) white fish fillets, skin on (such as snapper or barramundi)
1 tablespoon rice bran oil (or olive oil)
130 g (4½ oz/½ cup) low-fat Greek-style yoghurt

EGGPLANT AND POMEGRANATE SALAD

1 eggplant (aubergine), thinly sliced
60 ml (2 fl oz/¼ cup) balsamic vinegar
1 tablespoon honey
1 pomegranate
1 large handful rocket (arugula)
2 zucchini (courgettes), shaved into strips using a vegetable peeler
2 tablespoons pistachio nuts, roughly chopped
1 tablespoon olive oil
juice of 1 lemon

Heat a non-stick frying pan over high heat. Combine the cumin and coriander in a small bowl and coat the flesh side of each piece of fish with the mixture. Add the rice bran oil to the pan, then the fish, skin side down. Cook for 3–4 minutes on each side until the skin is crisp and the flesh is just starting to flake apart.

Remove the fish from the pan and set aside, lightly covered. Add the eggplant to the pan, in batches, adding another drizzle of oil if the pan looks dry. Cook for 1–2 minutes on each side until lightly golden brown, then add the balsamic vinegar and honey. Cook, turning regularly, for 2–3 minutes until the vinegar has reduced and the eggplant is cooked through. Set aside to cool slightly.

Cut the pomegranate in half. Hold the pomegranate cut side down over a large bowl and use a wooden spoon to repeatedly tap the pomegranate until all the seeds fall out. Combine with the rocket, zucchini strips, pistachios, eggplant, olive oil and lemon juice.

Transfer the spiced fish onto four serving plates with the eggplant and pomegranate salad. Serve with the yoghurt.

 NUTRITION TIP *Pomegranates are a great source of fibre, vitamin C and vitamin K.*

SUBSTITUTION *If pan-frying fish isn't your thing, consider oven-baking your fish wrapped in foil. It's super simple and hassle free. Purchase skinless fish though, as the skin will turn soggy and unpleasant in the steamy foil environment.*

NUTRITION INFORMATION (PER SERVE)	ENERGY	PROTEIN	SODIUM	FAT	SAT FAT	CARBOHYDRATE	SUGAR	FIBRE
	1552 kJ (371 cal)	28.7 g	115 mg	16.2 g	3.4 g	23.4 g	21.5 g	6.9 g

ISRAELI COUSCOUS, CHICKEN AND PUMPKIN SALAD WITH TAHINI YOGHURT

SERVES 4

Couscous is essentially tiny balls of refined wheat, which double in size when cooked. The couscous here absorbs the roasted flavours from the pumpkin and the sweet juices of the pomegranate, making a satisfying warm salad.

130 g (4½ oz) Israeli (pearl) couscous
375 ml (13 fl oz/1½ cups) salt-reduced chicken stock
1 tablespoon ground coriander
1 tablespoon allspice
2 x 250 g (9 oz) boneless, skinless chicken breasts, sliced into 1 cm (½ inch) thick pieces
1 tablespoon olive oil, plus 1 tablespoon extra
400 g (14 oz/about ½) butternut pumpkin (squash), peeled and cut into 1.5 cm (⅝ inch) dice
200 g (7 oz/1 head) broccoli, cut into florets
2 tablespoons pine nuts
½ small red onion, thinly sliced
2 handfuls baby spinach
seeds of ½ pomegranate (optional)
juice of 1 lemon
190 g (6¾ oz/⅔ cup) low-fat Greek–style yoghurt
1 tablespoon tahini

Combine the couscous and chicken stock in a saucepan. Bring to the boil over medium–high heat and cook for 8–10 minutes until tender. Drain well and set aside.

Combine the coriander and allspice in a large bowl and toss through the chicken slices to coat.

Heat 1 tablespoon of the olive oil in a wide frying pan over high heat, then add the chicken. Cook for 1–2 minutes on each side (in batches if necessary) until golden brown, fragrant and just cooked through. Remove the chicken from the pan, lightly cover and set aside.

Add the remaining tablespoon of oil and the diced pumpkin to the pan. Cook, stirring for 3–5 minutes until the pumpkin is tender. Add the broccoli and a splash of hot water and cook for a further 1 minute before adding the pine nuts for the final 30 seconds of cooking.

Combine the couscous, chicken, pumpkin mixture, red onion, baby spinach, pomegranate seeds, if using, and lemon juice in a large bowl. Divide among serving plates. Stir together the yoghurt and tahini, spoon over each plate and serve.

NUTRITION TIP *Always buy salt-reduced stock. It's healthier and helps you maintain control over the amount of salt in your dish.*

SUBSTITUTION *If you can't find Israeli (pearl) couscous, any other type of couscous will work. You can even substitute the couscous for quinoa, freekeh or pearl barley.*

NUTRITION INFORMATION (PER SERVE)	ENERGY 2145 kJ (512 cal)	PROTEIN 42.3 g	SODIUM 502 mg	FAT 17.0 g	SAT FAT 2.4 g	CARBOHYDRATE 42.2 g	SUGAR 14.5 g	FIBRE 9.5 g

YOGHURT-BASED DRESSINGS

ARE A HEALTHIER AND REFRESHING ALTERNATIVE TO MAYONNAISE-BASED DRESSINGS.

PORK, FIG AND BLUE CHEESE SALAD WITH HONEY BALSAMIC GLAZE

SERVES 4

Figs, blue cheese, pork and honey balsamic—what a heavenly match. The bitter radicchio plays a really important role in cutting through these classic, rich flavours to create an exciting, balanced dish.

4 figs, quartered
1 radicchio (or 2 witlof), leaves separated
½ fennel bulb, thinly sliced
1 French shallot, thinly sliced
30 g (1 oz/¼ cup) toasted walnuts,
    coarsely chopped
1 tablespoon rice bran oil (or olive oil)
2 tablespoons fennel seeds
4 x 150 g (5½ oz) pieces pork loin
    or fillet
60 ml (2 fl oz/¼ cup) balsamic vinegar
2 tablespoons honey
2 tablespoons extra virgin olive oil
juice of 1 lemon
60 g (2¼ oz) blue cheese

Combine the figs, radicchio, fennel, shallot and walnuts in a large bowl.

Heat the rice bran oil in a non-stick frying pan over high heat. Press the fennel seeds and some salt into one side of the pork. Add the pork to the pan and cook for 3–4 minutes on each side until a deep golden brown and cooked to your liking. Remove from the pan and leave to rest, lightly covered.

Pour the balsamic vinegar and honey into the pan and return to a high heat. Cook for a minute or until the boiling bubbles reduce to indicate a light syrup has formed. Remove the pan from the heat and leave to cool for 2–3 minutes. Cut the pork into thick slices.

Toss the olive oil and lemon juice through the fig salad. Crumble over the blue cheese. Divide the salad among four plates, top with the pork and drizzle over the honey balsamic glaze and serve.

 NUTRITION TIP *A common misconception is that pork is a high-fat meat. While this is true of cuts like pork belly, fillets and cutlets are actually very lean. In fact, per 100 g, pork has slightly less kilojoules (calories) than chicken breast.*

SUBSTITUTION *Blue cheese is an acquired taste. If it's not for you, try feta cheese or capers.*

NUTRITION INFORMATION (PER SERVE)	ENERGY 1900 kJ (454 cal)	PROTEIN 39.3 g	SODIUM 268 mg	FAT 23.8 g	SAT FAT 5.9 g	CARBOHYDRATE 19.4 g	SUGAR 17.6 g	FIBRE 4.3 g

BAKED FISH WITH PUMPKIN, BASIL SAUCE AND FETA

SERVES 4

This dish is a fantastic stress-free way to prepare fish. The cooking takes place in the oven, so all you need to do is add ingredients at the right time. Tidy as you go, and then put your feet up and relax at the end of the meal.

700 g (1 lb 9 oz/about ½) kent or jap pumpkin (winter squash), cut into large wedges

2 tablespoon olive oil, plus 2 tablespoons extra

1 teaspoon freshly grated nutmeg

3 handfuls green beans, topped and tailed

10 thyme sprigs, leaves picked

zest and juice of 2 lemons

4 x 150 g (5½ oz) thick fish fillets (such as barramundi or salmon)

40 g (1½ oz/¼ cup) pepitas (pumpkin seeds)

2 handfuls basil, leaves picked

1 small garlic clove

80 g (2¾ oz) feta cheese

Preheat the oven to 200°C (400°F/Gas 6).

Toss the pumpkin, olive oil and nutmeg together in a bowl, then place on a large baking tray, or in a roasting dish. Transfer to the oven and roast for 30–40 minutes until golden brown and tender.

Meanwhile, place the beans on a baking tray, then top with the thyme leaves, the juice and zest of 1 lemon and finally, the fish.

While the pumpkin cooks for its final 15 minutes add the pepitas to the pumpkin tray and place the beans and fish in the oven—the fish should take about 15 minutes to cook.

While the fish cooks, combine three-quarters of the basil leaves, the garlic and the remaining lemon zest and juice in a small food processor and blitz until smooth. Stir through the remaining oil.

Check the fish—if it flakes apart it is ready. Remove both trays from the oven and transfer the pumpkin, pepitas, beans and fish onto a serving dish. Spoon over the basil sauce, crumble over the feta, top with the remaining basil leaves and serve.

NUTRITION TIP *Making your own sauces and dips is a great way to regulate your salt, sugar and fat intake.*

SUBSTITUTION *For fussy eaters, replace a piece of fish with chicken. You may need to give it a head-start in the oven.*

NUTRITION INFORMATION (PER SERVE)	ENERGY 2143 kJ (512 cal)	PROTEIN 41.2 g	SODIUM 340 mg	FAT 26.3 g	SAT FAT 6.7 g	CARBOHYDRATE 20.1 g	SUGAR 13.1 g	FIBRE 12.0 g

REVERSE-MARINATED BEEF WITH HORSERADISH YOGHURT AND LENTIL SALAD

SERVES 4

'What is a reverse marinade?' we hear you ask. Well, it's when you coat your meat in a delicious marinade after it has been cooked, of course!

LENTIL SALAD

2 beetroot (beets)
1 small fennel bulb, cut into
　1 cm (½ inch) wedges
1 tablespoon olive oil, plus
　1 tablespoon extra
40 g (1½ oz/¼ cup) almonds
105 g (3½ oz/½ cup) lentils
2 oranges
2 tablespoons apple cider vinegar
1 long red chilli, seeded and thinly sliced
2 handfuls dill, leaves roughly chopped
2 tablespoons capers, rinsed

1 tablespoon rice bran oil (or olive oil)
2 x 180 g (6½ oz) beef steaks
　(such as scotch fillet or sirloin)
70 g (2½ oz/¼ cup) low-fat
　Greek-style yoghurt
2 tablespoons store-bought horseradish

Preheat the oven to 180°C (350°F/Gas 4). Individually wrap the beetroot in foil, place on a baking tray and roast for 1 hour or until tender when pierced with a knife. Toss the fennel in 1 tablespoon of the olive oil. Add the fennel to the tray for the final 30 minutes of cooking. Add the almonds to the tray for the final 10 minutes, to toast. Remove from the oven and set aside until cool enough to handle.

Put the lentils in a saucepan, cover with plenty of hot water and bring to the boil over high heat. Boil for 20–25 minutes until tender. Drain and set aside in a bowl. Heat the rice bran oil in a non-stick frying pan over high heat. Add the beef and cook for 3–4 minutes per side until cooked to your liking.

Meanwhile, cut the oranges into segments and add to the lentils. Squeeze any leftover orange juice into a bowl and add the apple cider vinegar, remaining olive oil, the chilli and about three-quarters of the dill. Spoon half the dressing onto a chopping board and rest the steaks on top.

Stir the yoghurt and horseradish together in a small bowl and set aside. Peel the beetroot—the skin should slip off now it is roasted—and cut into wedges. Add to the lentils, along with the fennel, toasted almonds, capers and the remaining dressing. Stir, then divide among four serving plates. Slice the steak and add to the plates. Spoon over the horseradish yoghurt, top with the remaining dill leaves and serve.

 NUTRITION TIP *Beetroot is a rich source of iron and folate and vitamins A, C and K.*

SUBSTITUTION *Instead of beef, use kangaroo, which is super lean.*

NUTRITION INFORMATION (PER SERVE)	ENERGY	PROTEIN	SODIUM	FAT	SAT FAT	CARBOHYDRATE	SUGAR	FIBRE
	2420 kJ (578 cal)	43.8 g	197 mg	32.5 g	8.4 g	23.5 g	13.0 g	9.9 g

BEETROOT AND GOAT'S CHEESE RISOTTO WITH FENNEL AND ORANGE SALAD

SERVES 4

This big beautiful pink risotto is earthy, rich and creamy, and partnered with the fresh zesty fennel and orange salad it makes a delicious vegetarian dish.

4 beetroot (beets)
40 g (1½ oz/¼ cup) pine nuts
1 litre (35 fl oz/4 cups) salt-reduced chicken or vegetable stock
1 tablespoon olive oil
1 brown onion, finely diced
4 garlic cloves, thinly sliced
3 handfuls basil, leaves picked, stems finely chopped
220 g (7¾ oz/1 cup) arborio rice
80 ml (2½ fl oz/⅓ cup) dry white wine
60 g (2¼ oz) goat's cheese, crumbled

FENNEL AND ORANGE SALAD

1 small fennel bulb
2 oranges
2 teaspoons apple cider vinegar (or lemon juice)
1 tablespoon olive oil

Preheat the oven to 200°C (400°F/Gas 6). Individually wrap the beetroot in foil, place on a tray and roast for 1 hour or until tender when pierced with a knife. Add the pine nuts to the tray for the final 5 minutes of cooking, to toast. Remove from the oven and set aside to cool. Put the stock in a saucepan and bring almost to the boil, then remove from the heat.

Heat the olive oil in a large, heavy-based saucepan over medium–low heat. Add the onion, garlic and basil stems, and cook gently, stirring occasionally, for 1–2 minutes until the onion is translucent. Add the rice, increase the heat to high, then add the wine. Once the wine bubbles away add the stock, a splash at a time, waiting for each addition of stock to be absorbed before adding the next. This process will take about 16–18 minutes. Stir occasionally. If you run out of stock and the rice needs a little more cooking, then add a little hot water. Meanwhile, put on some disposable gloves and peel the beetroot—the skin should slip off. Dice the beetroot and reserve.

To make the salad, thinly slice the fennel, segment (or peel and slice) the oranges and combine in a bowl. Dress with the apple cider vinegar and olive oil and set aside to serve. Stir the beetroot into the rice to stain the rice pink. Transfer the risotto into four serving bowls, top with the goat's cheese, toasted pine nuts and the basil leaves, and serve with the fennel and orange salad.

NUTRITION TIP *Bulk the risotto rice out with vegetables.*

SUBSTITUTION *If you are looking for a low-GI, higher fibre alternative, consider using quinoa or pearl barley instead of rice.*

NUTRITION INFORMATION (PER SERVE)	ENERGY	PROTEIN	SODIUM	FAT	SAT FAT	CARBOHYDRATE	SUGAR	FIBRE
	2116 kJ (506 cal)	12.5 g	1153 mg	21.2 g	4.4 g	59.8 g	14.1 g	9.5 g

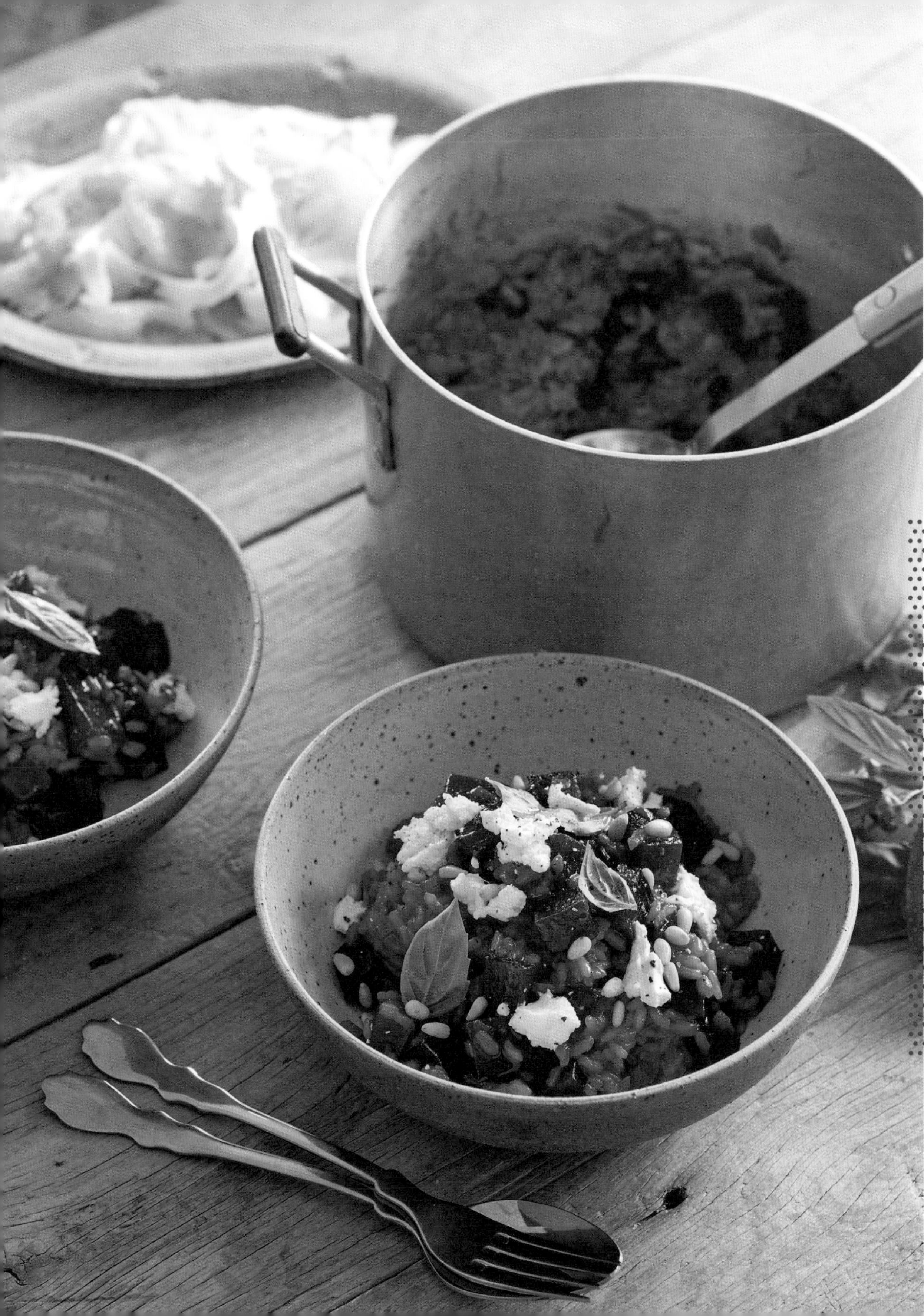

CHORIZO, TOMATO AND EGGPLANT ORECCHIETTE

SERVES 4

This dish uses the spices in the chorizo sausage and the eggplant to flavour the sauce. The additional chilli and spices take the sauce to the next level and the basil adds a fresh touch at the end.

1 tablespoon olive oil

1 chorizo sausage, halved lengthways, then thinly sliced

1 small eggplant (aubergine), cut into 1 cm (½ inch) dice

2 baby (pattypan) squash, quartered

1 brown onion, diced

3 garlic cloves, thinly sliced

1 long red chilli, thinly sliced

2 teaspoons allspice

3 handfuls basil, leaves picked, stems finely chopped

800 g (1 lb 12 oz) tinned chopped tomatoes

250 g (9 oz) orecchiette or other short pasta

30 g (1 oz) parmesan cheese

Heat the olive oil in a large saucepan over high heat. Add the chorizo and eggplant and cook, stirring occasionally, for 3–5 minutes until the chorizo is golden brown on both sides. Stir in the squash, onion, garlic, chilli, allspice and basil stems, then cook for a further 2–3 minutes until the mixture is fragrant and the onion has softened. Add the tomatoes and bring to the boil. Reduce the heat to medium and cook, stirring regularly, for 10–15 minutes until the sauce has reduced and darkened slightly in colour.

Cook the orecchiette in plenty of boiling water according to the packet directions until *al dente*. Drain the pasta, reserving about 80 ml (2½ fl oz/⅓ cup) of the cooking water. Toss the pasta and cooking water through the sauce. Divide among four pasta bowls, grate over the parmesan, top with the basil leaves and serve.

 NUTRITION TIP *Everyone enjoys a bowl of pasta and there is no need to avoid it or remove it from your diet. Instead just be aware of your portion size. Enjoy one cup of cooked pasta with a fresh vegetable-rich sauce and a side salad. Pasta should be one part of a meal, not the only part of a meal, much like red meat, chicken or fish.*

SUBSTITUTION *Orecchiette means 'small ear' in Italian. The shape captures and holds the sauce that it's served with. If you don't have orecchiette, your favourite pasta will be just as delicious.*

NUTRITION INFORMATION (PER SERVE)	ENERGY 1850 kJ (442 cal)	PROTEIN 19.2 g	SODIUM 453 mg	FAT 12.5 g	SAT FAT 3.7 g	CARBOHYDRATE 57.1 g	SUGAR 11.6 g	FIBRE 11.1 g

CHORIZO SAUSAGE IS A PORK-BASED SAUSAGE FLAVOURED USING SPICES SUCH AS PAPRIKA. IT CAN BE HIGH IN FAT BUT

IT'S ALSO FULL OF FLAVOUR, SO ONE SAUSAGE GOES A LONG WAY.

PAPRIKA LAMB WITH ROMESCO SAUCE AND CHILLI BEANS

SERVES 4

Romesco sauce is a Spanish chilli, capsicum and roasted nut sauce.
It's bright orange-red and usually accompanies seafood. However,
it's a versatile sauce and also works very well with lamb and poultry.
Give this recipe a try, it's one of our favourite dishes.

100 g (3½ oz/½ cup) roasted
  capsicum (pepper) pieces
40 g (1½ oz/¼ cup) roasted almonds,
  roughly chopped
1 garlic clove
1 teaspoon smoked paprika,
  plus 1 tablespoon extra
1 teaspoon ground cumin
90 ml (3 fl oz) tomato passata
  (puréed tomatoes)
zest and juice of 1 lemon
2 tablespoons olive oil, plus
  1 tablespoon extra
400 g (14 oz) lamb cutlets (or lamb
  backstrap or loin chops)
4 large handfuls green beans,
  topped and tailed
½ teaspoon chilli flakes
8 anchovy fillets, finely chopped
  (optional)

To make the romesco sauce, combine the capsicum, half the
almonds, garlic, 1 teaspoon of the paprika, cumin, tomato passata
and half the lemon juice in a food processor. Blend until smooth,
add the 2 tablespoons of olive oil and blend briefly to combine.

Heat the remaining oil in a large frying pan over high heat. Coat the
lamb in the remaining tablespoon of paprika, season with a pinch of
salt, then add to the pan. Cook for 2–3 minutes on each side until a
deep golden brown and cooked to your liking. Remove the lamb from
the pan and leave to rest, lightly covered.

Add the beans, chilli flakes and anchovies, if using, to the pan and cook
for about 2 minutes until bright green and slightly tender. Transfer into
a bowl and toss with the lemon zest and remaining juice. Divide the
beans among four serving plates. Top with the lamb, romesco sauce
and the remaining almonds and serve.

 NUTRITION TIP *Anchovies are a quick, easy and affordable source
of omega-3 fats, protein, calcium and iron. Depending on how they
are packaged, they can also be very salty, so it is good to give
them a rinse.*

SUBSTITUTION *If you like it hot, add a chilli to the romesco sauce
for a real kick. The spicy and sweet romesco sauce is a perfect
addition to Mexican tacos.*

NUTRITION INFORMATION (PER SERVE)	ENERGY	PROTEIN	SODIUM	FAT	SAT FAT	CARBOHYDRATE	SUGAR	FIBRE
	2145 kJ (512 cal)	28.0 g	621 mg	39.6 g	11.9 g	7.9 g	4.8 g	7.3 g

'NO-PROVE' PUMPKIN PIZZA

SERVES 4

Want your pizza, but hate the wait time? This is just the recipe for you!
By the time your takeaway pizza is delivered, this fresh homemade
delight could be on the table. The yoghurt base is light and fluffy and
a perfect match for sweet golden roasted vegetables.

1 tablespoon olive oil
200 g (7 oz/about ¼) butternut
   pumpkin (squash), peeled and
   cut into 1.5 cm (⅝ inch) dice
8 button mushrooms, thinly sliced
2 handfuls baby spinach
100 g (3½ oz/⅔ cup) self-raising flour,
   plus extra for dusting (gluten-free
   flour works just as well here)
95 g (3¼ oz/⅓ cup) low-fat
   Greek–style yoghurt
2 teaspoons dried oregano
1 x quantity beetroot–walnut purée
   (see page 136)
220 g (7¾ oz/1 cup) chopped marinated
   artichokes, drained well (optional)
80 g (2¾ oz) fresh mozzarella cheese,
   torn into bite-sized chunks

Heat the olive oil in a large frying pan over high heat. Add the pumpkin
and cook for 4–5 minutes, turning, until lightly golden and tender.
Remove from the pan and repeat the process with the mushrooms.
Return the pumpkin to the pan along with the baby spinach, and stir
until the spinach wilts. Remove the pan from the heat and cover lightly
to keep warm.

Mix the flour, yoghurt and oregano in a bowl using a spatula, then use
your hands to bring the dough together. Divide the mixture into four
pieces and dust each piece with a little extra flour. Use your fingers
to press each piece down into a thin circular shape to make four mini
pizzas. Cook each pizza base in a hot, dry frying pan for 1–2 minutes
on each side until golden brown.

Place the pizza bases on serving plates. Top with the beetroot–
walnut purée, pumpkin mixture, artichokes, if using, and mozzarella,
then serve.

 NUTRITION TIP *Use wholemeal flour to increase the fibre
content of the pizza and lower the GI.*

SUBSTITUTION *If you need to make this pizza base gluten-free,
substitute the wheat flour for gluten-free flour. The result is great
as the yoghurt adds a thick moist texture usually missing from
gluten-free products.*
Instead of beetroot–walnut purée, you could use pesto or hummus.

NUTRITION INFORMATION (PER SERVE)	ENERGY	PROTEIN	SODIUM	FAT	SAT FAT	CARBOHYDRATE	SUGAR	FIBRE
	1807 kJ (432 cal)	19.1 g	471 mg	22.6 g	6.9 g	32.5 g	12.1 g	10.7 g

BAKLAVA-STUFFED FIGS

SERVES 4

Baklava is a Middle Eastern dessert characterised by layers of pastry, nuts and a sweet honey syrup. It's traditionally an energy-dense sweet, which is fine if you're planning on running a marathon, but we've come up with a healthier option here in case a quiet night in front of the telly is more your thing.

35 g (1¼ oz) walnuts, roughly chopped
40 g (1½ oz/¼ cup) almonds,
   roughly chopped
1 teaspoon ground cinnamon
finely grated zest and juice of 1 lemon
90 g (3¼ oz/¼ cup) honey
1 teaspoon vanilla bean paste
1 tablespoon rosewater (optional)
4 figs

Combine the walnuts and almonds in a hot, dry frying pan and toast for 1–2 minutes until lightly fragrant. Remove from the heat and stir in the cinnamon. Tip into a small bowl and set aside.

Combine the lemon zest and juice, honey, vanilla bean paste, rosewater, if using, and 60 ml (2 fl oz/¼ cup) of water in a small saucepan. Bring to the boil, then set aside to cool slightly.

Score the top of the figs with a big 'X', then squeeze the bottom of each fig to help it open up. Spoon the toasted nut mixture onto each fig, drizzle with the syrup and serve.

NUTRITION TIP *Stir the vanilla bean paste through some natural yoghurt to add a calcium boost to this dessert, too.*

SUBSTITUTION *Swap figs for summer fruits, such as peaches or apricots for a delicious summer dessert.*

NUTRITION INFORMATION (PER SERVE)	ENERGY 935 kJ (223 cal)	PROTEIN 4.1 g	SODIUM 6 mg	FAT 11.7 g	SAT FAT 0.8 g	CARBOHYDRATE 23.8 g	SUGAR 23.7 g	FIBRE 3.7 g

YOGHURT AND ROSEWATER PANNA COTTA WITH ROASTED PERSIMMONS

SERVES 6

Panna cotta is an Italian dessert, which translated means 'cooked cream'. We've used 50 per cent low-fat yoghurt which adds a pleasant acidity as well as making for a healthier dessert. The roasted persimmons then provide a sweetness to round out the dish.

250 ml (9 fl oz/1 cup) low-fat thin (pouring) cream
55 g (2 oz/¼ cup) caster (superfine) sugar
2 gold-strength gelatine leaves
260 g (9¼ oz/1 cup) low-fat Greek-style yoghurt
1 tablespoon rosewater
4 persimmons, skin removed and cut into wedges
1 tablespoon honey
¼ teaspoon ground cinnamon
3 tablespoons pistachio nuts, chopped

Place the cream and sugar in a small saucepan over medium heat. Heat, stirring occasionally, until the sugar has dissolved.

Meanwhile, soak the gelatine leaves in cold water for a minute or until soft. Remove the saucepan from the heat and add the softened gelatine. Whisk until the gelatine has dissolved. Whisk in the yoghurt and rosewater.

Divide the yoghurt mixture among six serving glasses or lightly greased moulds. Place in the fridge for 2–3 hours until set.

Preheat the oven to 190°C (375°F/Gas 5). Line a baking tray with baking paper.

Toss the persimmon wedges, honey and cinnamon together in a bowl and place on the prepared tray. Roast for 10–15 minutes until golden brown. The persimmons can either be used warm or cooled.

Remove the panna cotta from the fridge and serve immediately, topped with the persimmon wedges and a scattering of pistachios.

 NUTRITION TIP *Spices such as vanilla, cinnamon and nutmeg, and ingredients like rosewater add flavour to a dish and perceived sweetness without adding extra sugar.*

SUBSTITUTION *If persimmons are hard to come by, try fresh or roasted figs instead.*

NUTRITION INFORMATION (PER SERVE)	ENERGY 1251 kJ (299 cal)	PROTEIN 5.9 g	SODIUM 46 mg	FAT 12.6 g	SAT FAT 6.7 g	CARBOHYDRATE 40.2 g	SUGAR 38.6 g	FIBRE 3.5 g

ROSEWATER IS MADE BY STEEPING ROSE PETALS IN WATER. **IT IS FREQUENTLY USED IN GREEK, TURKISH AND PERSIAN DISHES** AND IS WELL KNOWN FOR ITS USE IN TURKISH DELIGHT.

ORANGE AND HONEY RICOTTA TEN-MINUTE BRÛLÉE

SERVES 4

Crème brûlée is essentially a baked custard topped with a dry caramel. Traditionally the custard is flavoured with vanilla and made using cream to create a thick, rich consistency. Our brûlée uses flavoured ricotta instead of custard, making it a lot healthier and one of the quickest and easiest desserts ever!

500 g (1 lb 2 oz) low-fat ricotta cheese (from a tub, not the deli section of your supermarket)
2 tablespoons honey
finely grated zest of 1 orange
2 teaspoons vanilla bean paste (or vanilla extract)
1 tablespoon caster (superfine) sugar

Preheat the grill (broiler) to high.

Combine the ricotta, honey, orange zest and vanilla bean paste in a bowl. Divide the mixture among four small ramekins and use the back of a spoon to smooth the tops. Sprinkle the caster sugar over the top, then grill for 5–7 minutes until the sugar bubbles and caramelises. Serve warm or cooled.

NUTRITION TIP *Try serving this dish with some roasted or poached fruit.*

SUBSTITUTION *If you don't have vanilla bean paste or extract, you could use the seeds from a fresh vanilla bean or even ½ teaspoon of ground cinnamon or freshly grated nutmeg.*

NUTRITION INFORMATION (PER SERVE)	ENERGY 871 kJ (208 cal)	PROTEIN 15.1 g	SODIUM 279 mg	FAT 7.4 g	SAT FAT 4.7 g	CARBOHYDRATE 19.4 g	SUGAR 19.4 g	FIBRE 0.4 g

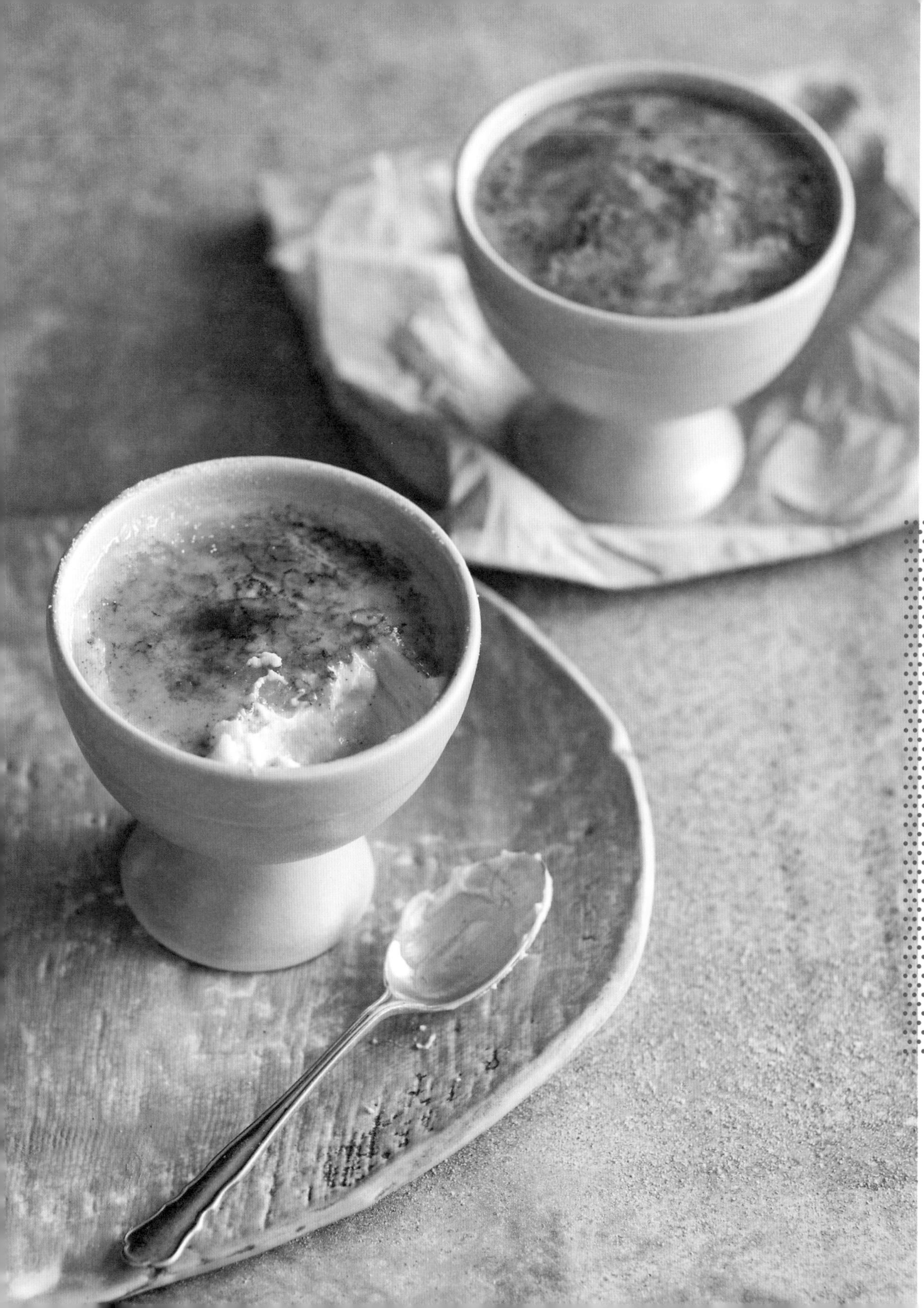

HONEY PEARS WITH ROSEMARY ORANGE CUSTARD AND GINGER CRUMBLE

SERVES 4

Infusing hard herbs and the zest of fruits into liquids is a great way to add flavour to a dish with no extra sugar, salt or fat and very little effort! The longer you leave the infusion the stronger the flavour will be.

zest and juice of 1 orange
375 ml (13 fl oz/1½ cups) low-fat milk
2 rosemary sprigs
2 teaspoons vanilla bean paste
   (or vanilla extract)
2 egg yolks
1 tablespoon honey, plus
   2 teaspoons extra
2 teaspoons cornflour (cornstarch)
2 tablespoons plain (all-purpose) flour
1 teaspoon ground ginger
2 teaspoons butter
1 tablespoon caster (superfine) sugar
¼ teaspoon ground cinnamon
30 g (1 oz) pecans, crumbled into
   small pieces by hand
4 pears
1 tablespoon olive oil

Put the orange zest in a saucepan with the milk, rosemary and vanilla bean paste. Reserve the juice. Bring to a simmer over medium heat, then remove from the heat and leave to infuse for 2–3 minutes.

Whisk the egg yolks, 1 tablespoon of the honey and the cornflour together in a bowl. Remove the rosemary and orange zest from the milk. Pour the hot milk mixture into the bowl with the egg yolks and whisk to combine. Pour the mixture back into the saucepan. Gently cook the custard over medium heat, whisking until thickened. Set aside.

Rub the flour, ginger, butter, sugar, cinnamon and pecans together in a small bowl. Tip the mixture into a dry frying pan and cook over medium–high heat for a few minutes, stirring, until golden and fragrant. Remove the crumble from the pan and set aside. Wipe out the pan.

Cut the pears into quarters, cut out the core from each quarter, then cut in half to yield eight pieces from each pear. Using the same pan used to toast the ginger crumble, heat the olive oil over medium heat. Add the pear pieces and cook for 2–3 minutes until golden. Add the reserved orange juice and the remaining honey. Toss to coat the pears. Cook for a further minute or until the pears soften slightly. Place the honey pears in a serving bowl, top with the ginger crumble and serve with the rosemary and orange custard.

NUTRITION TIP *Portion control is important when eating dessert. Make the pears the hero of the dish.*

SUBSTITUTION *Infuse the custard with lavender and lemon zest.*

NUTRITION INFORMATION (PER SERVE)	ENERGY	PROTEIN	SODIUM	FAT	SAT FAT	CARBOHYDRATE	SUGAR	FIBRE
	1497 kJ (358 cal)	6.8 g	65 mg	14.9 g	3.7 g	45.1 g	35.0 g	7.5 g

COCONUT SAGO PUDDING WITH PASSIONFRUIT AND MACADAMIAS

SERVES 4

Sago is a type of starch extracted from the trunk of the sago palm. Bought in the form of pearls, it has similar cooking and nutritional properties to rice. This pudding has a beautiful light texture, which is complemented by the fresh coconut and passionfruit flavours. A perfect autumn dessert.

150 g (5½ oz) sago
45 g (1½ oz) macadamia nuts
30 g (1 oz/½ cup) flaked coconut
60 ml (2 fl oz/¼ cup) coconut cream
2 tablespoons honey
4 passionfruit, pulp scooped out

Preheat the oven to 180°C (350°F/Gas 4).

Cook the sago in a large saucepan of boiling water for 10–15 minutes until clear and tender. Drain, rinse well under cold water to stop the cooking process, then drain again.

Meanwhile, place the macadamias and coconut on a baking tray. Transfer to the oven and bake for 8–12 minutes until golden brown and toasted. Remove from the oven and leave to cool.

Place the sago in a bowl and stir through the coconut cream and honey. Divide among four serving bowls. Top each with some of the passionfruit pulp and the toasted macadamias and coconut, and serve.

 NUTRITION TIP *Sago is almost 100 per cent carbohydrate, perfect for carbohydrate loading in the lead-up to a long endurance event.*

SUBSTITUTION *Macadamia nuts with passionfruit is a match made in heaven, but if you disagree, go ahead and use your favourite nut, perhaps hazelnuts.*

NUTRITION INFORMATION (PER SERVE)	ENERGY	PROTEIN	SODIUM	FAT	SAT FAT	CARBOHYDRATE	SUGAR	FIBRE
	1284 kJ (307 cal)	1.7 g	9 mg	12.2 g	4.1 g	45.7 g	13.7 g	3.8 g

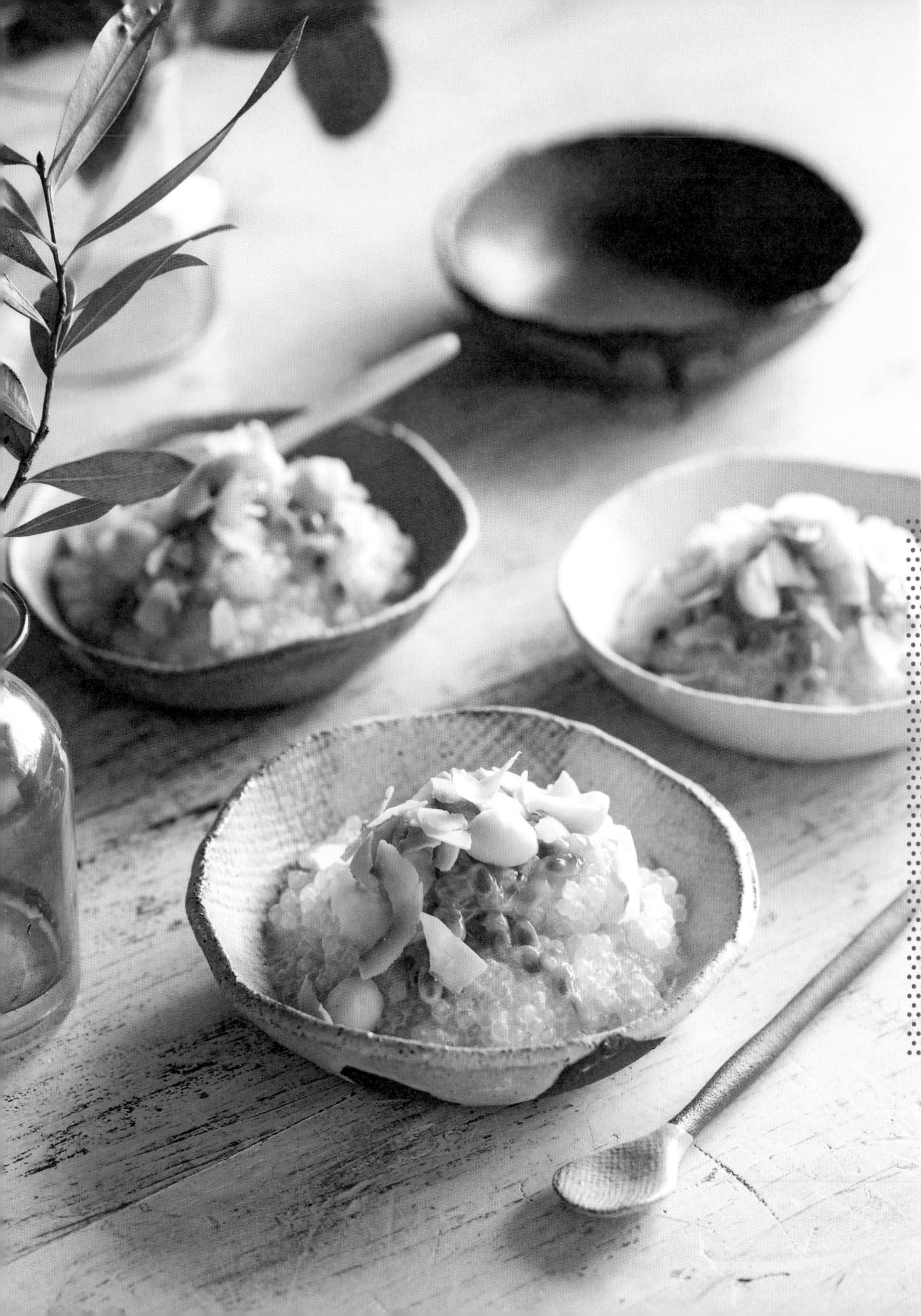

OPEN FIG TART

SERVES 4

We love a good fig—that sweet, jammy taste and soft, juicy texture.
It just breaks our hearts seeing backyards with figs rotting on the ground
in autumn. Here we've put beautiful, fresh figs to work, pairing them up
with golden pastry, mascarpone, honey yoghurt and pistachios.

1 sheet puff pastry, defrosted
85 g (3 oz/⅓ cup) mascarpone cheese
½ teaspoon ground cardamom (optional)
4 figs, sliced 5 mm (¼ inch) thick
1 tablespoon light brown sugar
1 teaspoon olive oil
2 tablespoons roughly chopped
   pistachio nuts
130 g (4½ oz/½ cup) low-fat
   Greek-style yoghurt
2 teaspoons honey

Preheat the oven to 190°C (375°F/Gas 5). Line a baking tray with baking paper.

Transfer the pastry onto the prepared baking tray. Using a paring knife, draw a border on the inside of the pastry, about 2 cm (¾ inch) from the edge. Mix the mascarpone and cardamom, if using, together, then spread over the pastry, keeping within the border. Lay the fig slices over the mascarpone. Evenly sprinkle over the brown sugar. Rub a little olive oil on the outside border of the pastry and drizzle any remaining oil over the figs. Bake for 20–25 minutes until the pastry is golden and has risen around the edges. Add the pistachios, sprinkled on top, for the final 5 minutes of baking.

Remove the fig tart from the oven. Cut into portions and transfer onto four serving plates. Stir together the yoghurt and honey. Drizzle over the fig tart and serve.

NUTRITION TIP *Compared to most tarts or pies, this dish has little pastry. However, don't let the light, flaky pastry fool you, it still packs a kilojoule (calorie) punch.*

SUBSTITUTION *This is a great last-minute dessert that is certain to impress your friends. If you are entertaining in the summer, try swapping the figs for peaches, plums or apricots.*

NUTRITION INFORMATION (PER SERVE)	ENERGY	PROTEIN	SODIUM	FAT	SAT FAT	CARBOHYDRATE	SUGAR	FIBRE
	1603 kJ (383 cal)	7.1 g	269 mg	25.1 g	13.3 g	31.6 g	13.3 g	2.8 g

WINTER

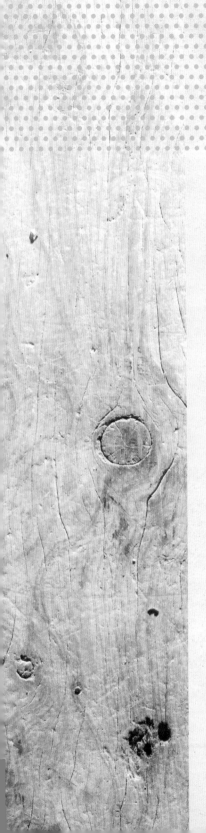

RICH.
COMFORTING.
FORTIFYING.

Winter is about escaping the elements and warding off all of those pesky winter bugs. The days are short, the nights are cold and all we want is to curl up next to a fire with a satisfying belly-filling soup, stew or casserole—dishes like our Fifteen-minute Vietnamese beef soup (page 132) or our Slow-cooked Moroccan lamb with cauliflower couscous (page 155).

Root vegetables flourish in winter—and they can stand up to the heavy style of food we crave at this time of year and absorb flavour while maintaining their colour and texture. These hardy vegetables also store well and are able to withstand the harsh winter weather.

WINTER SHOPPING LIST

Winter is about humble fruits and vegetables—those that can really stand up to the harsher elements as other produce becomes scarce. Potatoes are a great source of vitamin C and vitamin B6, which is important for protein and carbohydrate metabolism, and carrots and pumpkin are very good sources of vitamin A, which is important for a healthy immune system and vision.

Winter fruit is all about lemons, mandarins, oranges, grapefruit, kiwi fruit and all of the other wonderful citrus that feature in salads, juices and fruit bowls, and let's not forget apples, pears and bananas, too. Winter fruit may not be as spectacular as those from other seasons, but they provide us with valuable sources of vitamin C and fibre to help keep us full and fight off colds. All while contributing little in the way of kilojoules (calories), which is perfect as most of us enter hibernation.

VEGETABLES

- BEAN SPROUTS
- BEETROOT (BEETS)
- BROCCOLI
- BRUSSELS
  SPROUTS
- CABBAGE
- CARROTS
- CAULIFLOWER
- CELERIAC
- CELERY
- FENNEL
- JERUSALEM
  ARTICHOKES
- KALE
- KOHLRABI
- LEEKS
- MUSHROOMS
- OKRA
- ONIONS
- PARSNIPS
- POTATOES
- PUMPKIN
  (SQUASH)
- SILVERBEET
  (SWISS CHARD)
- SPINACH
- SWEDE
- SWEET POTATO
- TURNIPS
- WITLOF

FRUIT

- APPLES
- AVOCADOS
- BANANAS
- BLOOD ORANGES
- CARA CARA
  NAVEL ORANGES
- CUMQUATS
- CUSTARD APPLES
- DATES
- GRAPEFRUIT
- KIWI FRUIT
- LEMONS
- MANDARINS
- NASHI PEARS
- NAVEL ORANGES
- PASSIONFRUIT
- PEARS
- POMELO
- QUINCE
- RHUBARB
- TANGELOS

MOROCCAN SWEET POTATO, CHICKPEA AND CHICKEN SALAD

SERVES 4

This is a seriously satisfying salad. It's bulky, full of protein and low-GI carbohydrate and high in fibre, which will keep you going for hours. The best part is, because it is not overly leafy it stores well and doesn't go too soggy making it the perfect office lunch.

1 medium–large sweet potato, peeled and cut into 2 cm (¾ inch) pieces
1 small red onion, cut into thin wedges
400 g (14 oz) tinned chickpeas, rinsed and drained
1 tablespoon olive oil, plus 1 tablespoon extra
1 tablespoon smoked paprika
40 g (1½ oz/¼ cup) pepitas (pumpkin seeds)
8 chicken tenderloins (about 450 g/1 lb in total)
1 tablespoon ground cumin
1 tablespoon dijon mustard
zest and juice of 1 lemon
40 g (1½ oz/¼ cup) currants
3 handfuls coriander (cilantro), leaves picked

Preheat the oven to 190°C (375°F/Gas 5). Line a baking tray with baking paper.

Place the sweet potato in a bowl with the onion wedges and chickpeas. Add the olive oil and smoked paprika and toss to coat, then roast for 25–30 minutes or until golden brown and tender. Add the pepitas to the tray for the final 5 minutes of cooking time, to toast. Set aside to cool.

Meanwhile, combine the chicken tenderloins and ground cumin in a bowl. Transfer the chicken into a roasting dish and bake for 10–15 minutes until just cooked through.

Whisk the remaining olive oil, the mustard, lemon zest and juice together in a bowl.

Combine the sweet potato, onion, chickpeas, pepitas, chicken, currants and dressing in a large bowl. Divide among four serving plates, top with the coriander leaves and serve.

NUTRITION TIP *Chickpeas are a nutrition powerhouse. They are low in fat and a great source of protein, low-GI carbohydrate, fibre and various vitamins and minerals including folate and iron. A chickpea-based meal once a week is a healthy idea.*

SUBSTITUTION *Instead of chickpeas try lentils, kidney beans, cannellini beans or even broad (fava) beans in spring.*

NUTRITION INFORMATION (PER SERVE)	ENERGY 1618 kJ (387 cal)	PROTEIN 34.9 g	SODIUM 300 mg	FAT 13.7 g	SAT FAT 2.4 g	CARBOHYDRATE 27.7 g	SUGAR 11.7 g	FIBRE 7.2 g

SUMAC FISH WITH FENNEL–GRAPEFRUIT SALAD AND SWEET POTATO MASH

SERVES 4

Sumac is tangy in flavour and compared to other spices it's slightly more granulated. It's a versatile spice, lending itself well to savoury and sweet dishes. The sumac in this dish balances the rich fish and the salad provides a hit of freshness with the light sweet potato mash.

2 sweet potatoes
4 x 150 g (5½ oz) white fish fillets, skin on (such as snapper or barramundi)
1 tablespoon sumac
1 tablespoon rice bran oil (or olive oil)
1 large handful green beans, topped and tailed

FENNEL–GRAPEFRUIT SALAD
2 grapefruit
2 tablespoons olive oil
2 tablespoons red wine vinegar
1 small fennel bulb, sliced as thinly as possible
2 handfuls flat-leaf (Italian) parsley, leaves picked
60 g (2¼ oz/⅓ cup) Sicilian (green) olives, pitted
1 small red onion, thinly sliced

Preheat the oven to 200°C (400°F/Gas 6). Place the sweet potatoes, whole, onto a baking tray, transfer to the oven and roast for 1 hour or until very tender. Cut each sweet potato in half lengthways, scoop out the flesh into a bowl and mash until smooth. Set aside.

Heat a non-stick frying pan over high heat. Coat the flesh side of the fish in the sumac. Add the rice bran oil to the pan, then add the fish, skin side down. Cook for 2–3 minutes until golden brown, then turn over and add the green beans to the pan. Cook for a further 2–3 minutes or until the fish has just cooked and the beans are slightly tender. Remove the fish and beans to four serving plates.

Meanwhile, zest one grapefruit into a small bowl. Segment both grapefruit into a large bowl and set aside. Pour any leftover juice from the segmenting process into the zest bowl. Stir in the olive oil and red wine vinegar. Add the fennel, parsley, olives and red onion to the large bowl with the grapefruit segments and mix to combine. Stir in the vinegar dressing.

Divide the salad among the serving plates with the fish and beans, and serve with some sweet potato mash.

 NUTRITION TIP *Grapefruit is an excellent source of vitamin C and a good source of antioxidants.*

SUBSTITUTION *Sumac works very well with seafood. If you're feeling adventurous, try this recipe with scallops or prawns (shrimp).*

NUTRITION INFORMATION (PER SERVE)	ENERGY 1573 kJ (376 cal)	PROTEIN 33.8 g	SODIUM 363 mg	FAT 14.9 g	SAT FAT 2.4 g	CARBOHYDRATE 22.4 g	SUGAR 13.5 g	FIBRE 6.2 g

WINTER

FIFTEEN-MINUTE VIETNAMESE BEEF SOUP

Everyone loves a good soup in winter. The problem is many of these leave you slicing, dicing and heating for hours! This soup is different. It uses beef stock, cinnamon, star anise, ginger and garlic to build a deep layered broth. Top with some vegetables and beef, and dinner will be on the table in minutes!

500 ml (17 fl oz/2 cups) salt-reduced
   beef stock
4 star anise
2 cinnamon sticks (or 1½ teaspoons
   ground cinnamon)
2 teaspoons fish sauce
2 tablespoons light brown sugar
1 thumb-sized piece ginger, sliced
5 garlic cloves, crushed
200 g (7 oz) thin, flat rice noodles
6 bok choy (pak choy), quartered
400 g (14 oz) beef fillet
1 long red chilli, sliced as thinly
   as you can
2 handfuls bean sprouts, to serve
3 handfuls coriander (cilantro) or basil,
   leaves picked
1 lime, cut into wedges, to serve
hoisin sauce, to serve
chilli sauce, to serve (optional)

In the biggest saucepan or pot you own, combine the beef stock, star anise, cinnamon, fish sauce, brown sugar, ginger, garlic and 1 litre (35 fl oz/4 cups) of water. Bring to the boil over high heat, then reduce the heat so the stock is lightly simmering. Cook for 10–12 minutes to allow the flavours to infuse. Use a slotted spoon to remove all the solids and discard them. Reduce the heat to medium and leave to simmer.

Meanwhile, cook the noodles according to the packet directions, adding the quartered bok choy for the last 2 minutes of cooking. Drain the noodles and bok choy and divide among four bowls.

Slice the beef as thinly as you possibly can, and place on top of the noodles. Pour the hot soup over the noodles and beef (ensure the broth is really hot, as the beef is cooked through by the soup) and top with the chilli slices, bean sprouts and coriander or basil. Serve with lime wedges, hoisin sauce and chilli sauce, if using, on the side.

 NUTRITION TIP *A serve of red meat in this dish is 90–100 g when raw. Consuming small amounts of meat within a dish, rather than making it the hero, will help reduce your ingredient costs and saturated fat intake while still meeting your nutrient requirements.*

SUBSTITUTION *To make your own stock, use the leftover beef bones from your winter casseroles and any leftover vegetables, add a few herbs, top with plenty of water, then simmer for 2–3 hours. Strain the liquid and you have a delicious soup base.*

NUTRITION INFORMATION (PER SERVE)	ENERGY	PROTEIN	SODIUM	FAT	SAT FAT	CARBOHYDRATE	SUGAR	FIBRE
	1698 kJ (406 cal)	41.5 g	846 mg	16.7 g	6.4 g	20.0 g	8.5 g	5.0 g

CHICKEN SATAY SKEWERS WITH SHREDDED CARROT SALAD

SERVES 4

Everybody loves chicken satay. Unfortunately most people use pre-made sauces, which are often just fatty and salty. This dish shows you how easy it is to make your own sauces. It also makes use of winter vegetables and fruits in a much lighter way than typical heavy winter dishes.

SATAY SAUCE

1 tablespoon rice bran oil (or olive oil)
2 garlic cloves, finely chopped
1 long red chilli, halved lengthways and seeds removed, finely chopped
1 thumb-sized piece ginger, grated
handful coriander (cilantro), stems finely chopped, leaves reserved
2 teaspoons fish sauce (or light soy sauce)
1 tablespoon brown sugar
125 ml (4 fl oz/½ cup) low-fat coconut milk
50 g (1¾ oz/⅓ cup) roasted peanuts, roughly chopped

⅛ Chinese cabbage (wombok), finely sliced
2 carrots, julienned
2 granny smith apples, julienned
small handful mint, leaves picked
230 g (8½ oz/2 cups) bean sprouts
juice of 2 limes (or 1 lemon)
8 chicken tenderloins (about 450 g/1 lb in total)
2 teaspoons rice bran oil (or olive oil)

Soak 8 wooden skewers in a bowl of cold water while you make the sauce.

To make the satay sauce, heat the rice bran oil in a small saucepan over medium–high heat. Add the garlic, chilli, ginger and coriander stems. Cook, stirring, for a minute or until lightly browned. Add the fish sauce and sugar and cook for a further minute or until the sugar has dissolved and caramelises. Stir in the coconut milk and bring to the boil. Cook for 2–3 minutes until reduced. Stir in the peanuts and cook until the sauce thickens slightly. Remove from the heat.

Combine the Chinese cabbage, carrot, apple, mint leaves, reserved coriander leaves, bean sprouts and lime juice in a large bowl. Set aside.

Thread the chicken tenderloins onto the skewers. Heat the rice bran oil in a frying pan over high heat, add the skewers and cook for 1–2 minutes on each side until golden and just cooked through.

Serve the chicken skewers with the satay sauce and shredded carrot salad.

 NUTRITION TIP *The apples in this salad provide a source of carbohydrate. If you want to increase the carbohydrate content of this dish, try rice noodles or brown rice.*

SUBSTITUTION *If you like it hot, try adding another chilli or use a bird's eye chilli instead. You could use prawns instead of chicken.*

NUTRITION INFORMATION (PER SERVE)	ENERGY 1402 kJ (335 cal)	PROTEIN 32.0 g	SODIUM 324 mg	FAT 13.7 g	SAT FAT 4.0 g	CARBOHYDRATE 17.5 g	SUGAR 15.5 g	FIBRE 7.0 g

MUSHROOM AND GINGER SAN CHOY BOW

This dish is all about the aromatic ingredients—such as ginger, garlic, chilli, coriander—and the extra flavour they bring to the mushrooms. This vegetarian dish is perfect for the whole family, and the little ones will love being allowed to use their hands to eat.

1½ tablespoons rice bran oil (or olive oil)
800 g (1 lb 12 oz) mixed mushrooms, finely chopped
1 thumb-sized piece ginger, finely grated
1 long red chilli, seeded and thinly sliced
4 garlic cloves, finely chopped
2 handfuls coriander (cilantro), leaves picked, stems finely chopped
225 g (8 oz) tinned water chestnuts, drained and finely chopped
2 tablespoons hoisin sauce
130 g (4½ oz) bean sprouts
4 spring onions (scallions), thinly sliced on an angle
1 small cos (romaine) lettuce, leaves separated
1 tablespoon sesame seeds, to serve

Heat the rice bran oil in a large frying pan or wok over high heat. Add half the mushrooms. Cook, stirring, for 2–3 minutes until browned. Remove the mushrooms from the pan and repeat with the remaining mushrooms. Return all the mushrooms to the pan, then stir in the ginger, chilli, garlic and coriander stems. Cook for 2–3 minutes, then add the water chestnuts and hoisin sauce. Stir, then continue to cook until most of the liquid has evaporated. Remove from the heat, add the bean sprouts and spring onion to the pan and stir through.

Place 2 lettuce leaves on each of four plates. Divide the mushroom mixture among the lettuce leaves. Scatter over the coriander leaves and sesame seeds, and serve.

NUTRITION TIP *Jam a few extra vegies into this dish with some grated carrot and chopped spinach leaves.*
Consider using salt-reduced soy sauce instead of the hoisin to help reduce the sodium quantity of this dish.

SUBSTITUTION *If you feel the need to include some meat in this dish, then try adding pork mince in place of some of the mushrooms.*

NUTRITION INFORMATION (PER SERVE)	ENERGY	PROTEIN	SODIUM	FAT	SAT FAT	CARBOHYDRATE	SUGAR	FIBRE
	791 kJ (189 cal)	10.1 g	205 mg	10.2 g	1.4 g	10.3 g	6.6 g	8.9 g

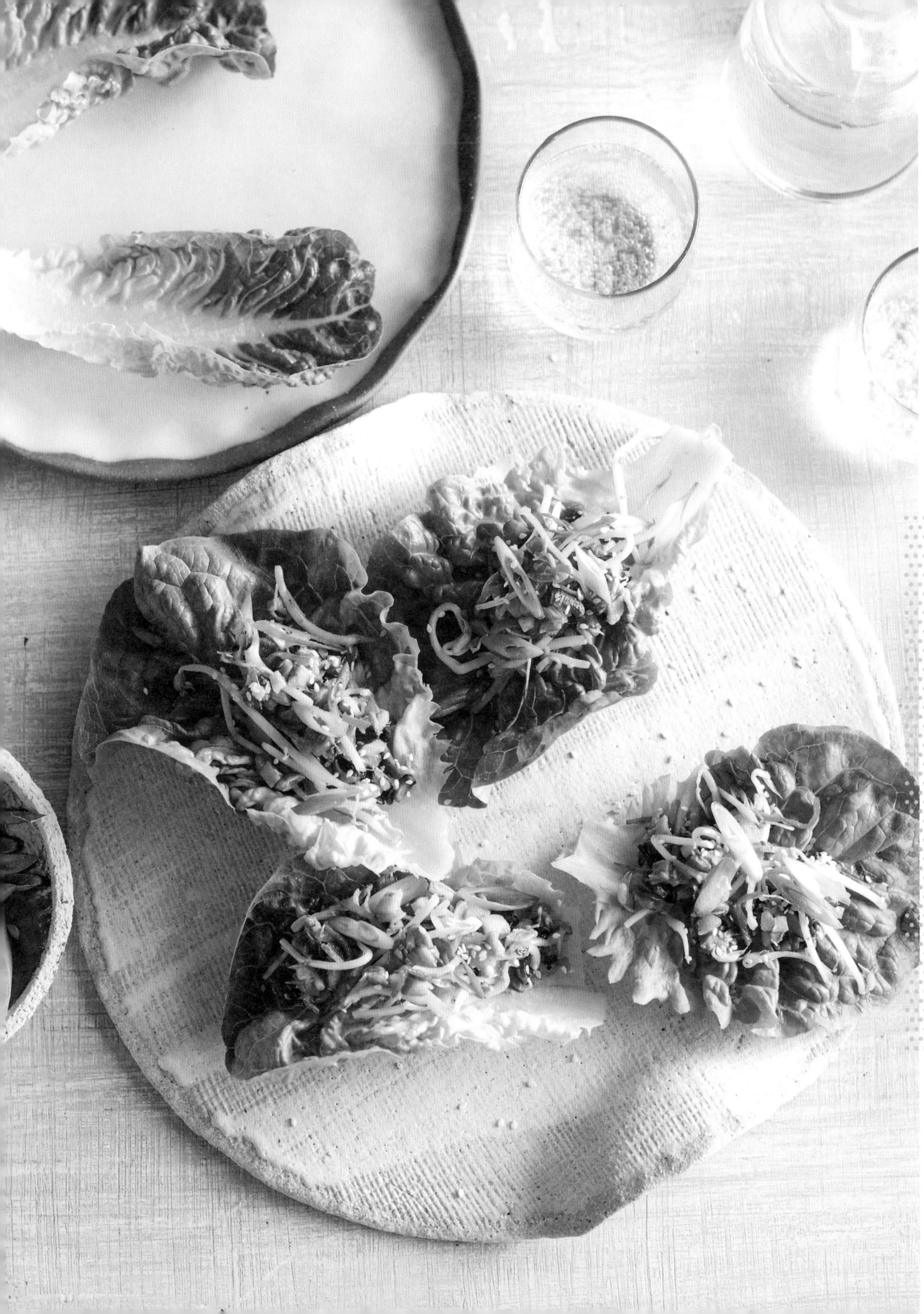

ROAST PUMPKIN AND LENTIL SALAD WITH BEETROOT–WALNUT PURÉE

You can't force people to eat more vegetables, but you can make them irresistible. The roast beetroot–walnut purée is colourful, earthy and creamy, and complements the roast vegetables perfectly.

BEETROOT–WALNUT PURÉE

2 beetroot (beets)

25 g (1 oz) walnuts, plus 25 g (1 oz) extra for the salad

95 g (3¼ oz/⅓ cup) low-fat Greek-style yoghurt

25 g (1 oz) creamy feta cheese, plus 25 g (1 oz) extra for the salad

2 tablespoons olive oil, plus 1 tablespoon extra

400 g (14 oz/about ½) butternut pumpkin (squash), peeled and cut into 2 cm (¾ inch) cubes

2 zucchini (courgettes), cut into 2 cm (¾ inch) pieces

3 garlic cloves, thinly sliced

1 small handful thyme, leaves picked

800 g (1 lb 12 oz) tinned lentils, rinsed and drained

1 pear, thinly sliced

3 handfuls rocket (arugula)

60 ml (2 fl oz/¼ cup) white balsamic vinegar or apple cider vinegar

Preheat the oven to 200°C (400°F/Gas 6). Individually wrap the beetroot in foil, place on a baking tray and roast for 1 hour or until tender when pierced with a knife. Add all the walnuts to the tray for the final 10 minutes of cooking time, to toast. Remove from the oven and set aside until cool enough to handle.

Meanwhile, combine 2 tablespoons of the olive oil, the pumpkin, zucchini, garlic and thyme in bowl. Toss together to coat everything in the oil. Transfer onto a large baking tray and put in the oven with the beetroot. Cook for 20–25 minutes until the pumpkin is golden brown and tender. Set aside to cool slightly.

To make the beetroot–walnut purée, put on some disposable gloves and peel the beetroot—the skins should slip off now they are roasted. Roughly chop, transfer to the bowl of a food processor and blend with the yoghurt, 25 g (1 oz) of the feta and 25 g (1 oz) of the toasted walnuts until smooth.

Combine the cooked pumpkin and zucchini in a bowl with the lentils, pear, rocket, remaining olive oil and the white balsamic vinegar. Divide the beetroot–walnut purée among four serving plates and top with the lentil mixture. Crumble over the remaining feta and walnuts and serve.

NUTRITION TIP *Serve this salad with a piece of lean protein, such as white fish, for a complete balanced meal.*

SUBSTITUTION *You can also use goat's cheese or, alternatively, some crumbled blue cheese in place of the feta.*

NUTRITION INFORMATION (PER SERVE)	ENERGY	PROTEIN	SODIUM	FAT	SAT FAT	CARBOHYDRATE	SUGAR	FIBRE
	1762 kJ (421 cal)	16.9 g	199 mg	21.7 g	4.1 g	32.1 g	17.5 g	13.2 g

GREEK LEMON, CHICKEN AND MINT SOUP

SERVES 4

This dish is a take on a Greek classic, avgolemono soup, which is usually made from chicken stock, lemon, eggs, chicken and rice. The fresh herbs and spring onions lift the dish and provide a light vibrant and satisfying winter soup.

2 tablespoons olive oil

5 spring onions (scallions), white parts roughly chopped, green tops thinly sliced

3 garlic cloves, sliced

2 x 250 g (9 oz) boneless, skinless chicken breasts

1.5 litres (52 fl oz/6 cups) salt-reduced chicken stock

60 g (2¼ oz) rice (or small pasta)

2 eggs

juice of 2 lemons

140 g (5 oz/1 cup) frozen peas

3 handfuls baby spinach

1 handful mint (or dill), leaves picked

Heat the olive oil in a large saucepan over high heat, then add the spring onion white stems and the garlic. Cook, stirring, for 2–3 minutes until the onions soften. Add the chicken breasts and cover with the stock. Bring to a gentle simmer and cook for 12–15 minutes until the chicken is just cooked.

Meanwhile, cook the rice in a saucepan with plenty of boiling water for 2 minutes less than the directions on the packet state. Drain well.

Remove the chicken from the stock and slice or shred the meat. Whisk the eggs in a heatproof bowl, then gradually whisk in the lemon juice. Whisk in a ladleful of the hot stock, then gradually whisk in another ladle or two. Whisk the egg mixture into the soup, return the chicken to the soup and add the rice, peas, spinach and half the mint. Cook over low heat for 1–2 minutes until the soup thickens slightly and the spinach has wilted.

Divide the soup among four bowls, top with the sliced green parts of the spring onions and the remaining mint leaves, and serve.

 NUTRITION TIP *Use a low-GI brown rice or other whole grain, such as barley, to provide long-lasting energy and increase the fibre content of the dish.*

SUBSTITUTION *Instead of peas and spinach, try celery and carrot. You could also add a scattering of feta just before serving.*

NUTRITION INFORMATION (PER SERVE)	ENERGY	PROTEIN	SODIUM	FAT	SAT FAT	CARBOHYDRATE	SUGAR	FIBRE
	1552 kJ (370 cal)	37.1 g	1627 mg	15.4 g	3.3 g	19.3 g	3.3 g	4.5 g

ADD ANOTHER DIMENSION TO YOUR SOUP

WITH A HANDFUL OF CRUSHED NUTS, A DOLLOP OF YOGHURT, OR A BUNCH OF TORN HERBS.

PUMPKIN, GINGER AND LEMONGRASS SOUP

SERVES 4

This Thai-inspired pumpkin soup is a refreshing change from an old favourite. The coriander, ginger and chilli add a pleasant complexity to this soup and the lemongrass provides a zesty and fragrant addition, which will leave your kitchen smelling like a fancy Thai restaurant.

1 tablespoon rice bran oil (or olive oil)

1 kg (2 lb 4 oz/about 1 large) butternut pumpkin (squash), peeled and cut into 3 cm (1¼ inch) pieces

1 brown onion, diced

3 handfuls coriander (cilantro), roots and stems sliced, leaves reserved

1 thumb-sized piece ginger, roughly chopped

4 garlic cloves, sliced

1 long red chilli, sliced

3 lemongrass stems, bruised

8 kaffir lime leaves (optional)

400 ml (14 fl oz) tinned low-fat coconut milk

1 litre (35 fl oz/4 cups) salt-reduced chicken or vegetable stock

crusty bread, to serve

Heat the rice bran oil in a large saucepan over high heat. Add the pumpkin and cook for 3–4 minutes until lightly golden. Add the onion, coriander, ginger, garlic and chilli. Cook for a further minute or until fragrant.

Stir in the lemongrass, kaffir lime leaves, if using, coconut milk and stock. Simmer the soup for 10–15 minutes or until the pumpkin is soft.

Remove the kaffir lime leaves and lemongrass, remove from the heat and purée the soup with a stick blender until smooth.

Divide the soup among four serving bowls, top with the coriander leaves and serve with crusty bread.

 NUTRITION TIP *Soups can be a great low-kilojoule meal option and provide a convenient way to increase your vegetable intake.*

SUBSTITUTION *Choose wholegrain bread. It's more satisfying and highly nutritious.*

NUTRITION INFORMATION (PER SERVE)	ENERGY	PROTEIN	SODIUM	FAT	SAT FAT	CARBOHYDRATE	SUGAR	FIBRE
	1121 kJ (268 cal)	6.9 g	1051 mg	13.6 g	7.4 g	26.1 g	18.4 g	9.1 g

CHICKEN KORMA WITH CUMIN NAAN

SERVES 4

Making your own curry paste allows you to take control of the heat, spice and salt content. Korma is a mildly spiced curry and is super simple to make, so give it a go.

130 g (4½ oz/½ cup) low-fat
  Greek-style yoghurt
3 garlic cloves, thinly sliced
1 thumb-sized piece ginger, finely grated
2 handfuls coriander (cilantro), stems
  finely chopped, leaves reserved
2 teaspoons garam masala, plus
  2 teaspoons extra
4 x 100 g (3½ oz) boneless, skinless
  chicken thighs
2 tablespoons rice bran oil (or olive oil)
1 brown onion, halved and thinly sliced
1 red capsicum (pepper), thinly sliced
2 teaspoons curry powder
250 ml (9 fl oz/1 cup) tomato passata
  (puréed tomatoes)
2 handfuls baby spinach

CUMIN NAAN BREAD
100 g (3½ oz/⅔ cup) self-raising flour,
  plus extra for dusting (gluten-free
  flour works just as well here)
95 g (3¼ oz/⅓ cup) low-fat
  Greek-style yoghurt
1 teaspoon cumin seeds
pinch of salt

Stir together the yoghurt, garlic, ginger, coriander stems and 2 teaspoons of the garam masala in a large bowl. Slice each chicken thigh into four pieces, then each of those into three pieces so you have twelve pieces per thigh. Stir the chicken into the yoghurt mixture and set aside to marinate.

Heat a large deep frying pan or stockpot over high heat. Add the rice bran oil, then add the onion and capsicum and stir for 2–4 minutes until the onion starts to become golden brown. Add the curry powder and the extra 2 teaspoons of garam masala. Cook for a 1–2 minutes, stirring until fragrant, before adding the chicken and yoghurt mixture. Cook for 2–3 minutes, stirring often until the yoghurt has started to brown. Stir in the passata and cook for a further 5–10 minutes until the chicken has cooked and the sauce has darkened slightly in colour.

Meanwhile, make the cumin naan bread. Mix the flour, yoghurt, cumin seeds and salt in a bowl using a spatula, then use your hands to bring the dough together. Divide the mixture into four and dust each piece with a little extra flour. Press each dough piece down into a thin circular shape. Heat a frying pan over high heat, add the naan, two at a time and cook for 1–2 minutes on each side until golden brown.

Stir the baby spinach through the chicken korma and top with the reserved coriander leaves. Serve the korma with the cumin naan.

 NUTRITION TIP *Curries are a great way to increase vegetable intake, as the vegetables absorb the flavour of the dish.*

SUBSTITUTION *Try substituting prawns for the chicken.*

NUTRITION INFORMATION (PER SERVE)	ENERGY	PROTEIN	SODIUM	FAT	SAT FAT	CARBOHYDRATE	SUGAR	FIBRE
	2033 kJ (486 cal)	25.2 g	410 mg	28.7 g	6.4 g	29.2 g	8.9 g	4.8 g

LAMB WITH THYME MUSHROOMS, PEARL BARLEY AND GOAT'S CHEESE

SERVES 4

Every element in this dish complements the others. The lean, tender juicy lamb, the earthy rich golden thyme mushrooms, the nutty chewy pearl barley and the tart goat's cheese—perfect for a cold winter's night.

140 g (5 oz/⅔ cup) pearl barley
1 tablespoon olive oil, plus
   1 tablespoon extra
2 x 200 g (7 oz) lamb backstraps
   (or lamb cutlets or loin chops)
500 g (1 lb 2 oz) mixed mushrooms,
   sliced
2 garlic cloves, sliced
6 thyme sprigs
1 tablespoon butter
2 handfuls baby spinach
2 tablespoons sherry vinegar
   (or red wine vinegar)
3 handfuls flat-leaf (Italian) parsley,
   roughly chopped
60 g (2¼ oz) goat's cheese, crumbled

Cook the pearl barley in a saucepan of boiling water over high heat for 20–25 minutes until tender. Drain well and set aside.

Heat 1 tablespoon of the olive oil in a large frying pan over high heat. Add the lamb to the pan. Cook for 3–4 minutes on each side or until golden brown and cooked to your liking. Remove from the pan and leave to rest, lightly covered.

Add a quarter of the mushrooms to the pan and fry for 2–3 minutes until golden brown on all sides. Remove the mushrooms from the pan and repeat with the remaining mushrooms. Return all the mushrooms to the pan. Add the garlic, thyme and butter and toss to coat. Add the baby spinach and stir until wilted.

Put the pearl barley in a large bowl and stir in the remaining olive oil, the sherry vinegar and most of the parsley. Slice the lamb.

Divide the pearl barley among four serving bowls. Top with the lamb and mushrooms. Scatter over the crumbled goat's cheese and remaining parsley and serve.

 NUTRITION TIP *Pearl barley is great to include to bulk up a dish because it is low GI and high in fibre.*

SUBSTITUTION *Can't find pearl barley? Try brown rice. No goat's cheese? Use feta. Don't do lamb? Try grilled chicken breast.*

NUTRITION INFORMATION (PER SERVE)	ENERGY 1910 kJ (456 cal)	PROTEIN 32.8 g	SODIUM 183 mg	FAT 23.3 g	SAT FAT 8.2 g	CARBOHYDRATE 24.2 g	SUGAR 1.1 g	FIBRE 8.7 g

PRAWNS WITH CELERIAC, BROCCOLI AND DILL SLAW

SERVES 4

Celeriac and fennel are really versatile winter vegetables, but unfortunately people look at these slightly less common vegies as creatures from outer space and don't dare attempt to cook with them. Come on. Trust us. Give this fresh, quick winter dish a go.

CELERIAC, BROCCOLI AND DILL SLAW
200 g (7 oz/1 head) broccoli, cut
    into 2 cm (¾ inch) florets
125 ml (4 fl oz/½ cup) buttermilk
2 tablespoons olive oil, plus
    1 tablespoon extra
zest and juice of 1 lemon
¼ teaspoon freshly ground black pepper
1 small celeriac, skin removed,
    flesh julienned
½ fennel bulb, thinly sliced
4 spring onions (scallions), thinly sliced
2 tablespoons capers, rinsed
2 handfuls dill, roughly chopped

24 large prawns (shrimp), peeled and
    deveined, leaving the tails intact

Bring a large saucepan half-filled with water to the boil over high heat. Add the broccoli and cook for 2 minutes or until bright green and tender-crisp. Drain in a colander, place in a bowl of cold water for 2 minutes to stop the cooking process, then drain again. Set aside.

In a large bowl, whisk together the buttermilk, 2 tablespoons of the olive oil, the lemon zest and juice, and pepper. Stir through the broccoli, celeriac, fennel, spring onion, capers and half the dill until combined.

Heat the remaining 1 tablespoon of oil in a frying pan over very high heat. Add the prawns and cook (in batches if necessary) for 30–60 seconds on each side until golden and just cooked.

Divide the slaw among four serving plates, top with the prawns and the remaining dill and serve.

 NUTRITION TIP *Buttermilk is actually not as unhealthy as it sounds. It refers to the liquid left behind after churning butter out of cream and is actually low in fat.*

SUBSTITUTION *Include a carrot or red cabbage in the slaw for extra colour.*
If you can't find buttermilk, try using low-fat Greek-style yoghurt instead.

NUTRITION INFORMATION (PER SERVE)	ENERGY	PROTEIN	SODIUM	FAT	SAT FAT	CARBOHYDRATE	SUGAR	FIBRE
	1187 kJ (284 cal)	29.3 g	524 mg	13.1 g	2.5 g	8.1 g	6.6 g	7.9 g

WHITE FISH WITH PUMPKIN QUINOA AND HERB YOGHURT

SERVES 4

Quinoa, like most grains and seeds, is not very exciting by itself. However, it carries other flavours really well. Don't make the quinoa the hero of the meal, but rather the flavour transporter.

100 g (3½ oz/½ cup) quinoa
3 handfuls flat-leaf (Italian) parsley
1 handful dill, leaves picked (optional)
1 garlic clove, roughly chopped
zest and juice of 1 lemon
130 g (4½ oz/½ cup) low-fat
    Greek-style yoghurt
1 tablespoon rice bran oil (or olive oil)
4 x 150 g (5½ oz) white fish fillets, skin
    on (such as snapper or barramundi)
300 g (10½ oz/about ¼) butternut
    pumpkin (squash), peeled and cut
    into 1 cm (½ inch) cubes
2 handfuls spinach leaves (or silverbeet/
    Swiss chard), roughly chopped
2 tablespoons pine nuts
½ red onion, thinly sliced
2 tablespoons currants
1 tablespoon olive oil

Put the quinoa in a saucepan and cover with plenty of water. Bring to the boil and cook for 13–15 minutes until tender. Drain and set aside. Put half the parsley, the dill, if using, garlic, lemon zest and yoghurt in a food processor and blitz until well combined. Alternatively, chop the herbs and garlic together, then stir in the remaining ingredients. Set aside.

Heat a large, heavy-based frying pan over medium–high heat. Add the rice bran oil. Season the fish with salt, then place the fillets in the pan, skin side down. Cook for 2–3 minutes, until golden brown, then turn over, reduce the heat to medium–low and cook gently for a further 1–3 minutes (depending on the thickness) until just cooked through. Remove from the pan, lightly cover, and set aside.

Add the pumpkin to the pan and cook for 2–3 minutes until the pumpkin is almost tender. Add the spinach, cook for a further 2 minutes, then add the pine nuts. Stir for a minute to toast, then remove the pan from the heat.

Combine the quinoa, pumpkin mixture, remaining parsley, onion, currants, lemon juice and olive oil in a bowl. Divide among four serving plates, top with the fish, spoon over the herbed yoghurt and serve.

 NUTRITION TIP *Quinoa is not only a gluten free alternative to many other grains, it also provides a complete source of protein.*

SUBSTITUTION *Try swapping the pumpkin for diced sweet potato or quartered brussels sprouts.*

NUTRITION INFORMATION (PER SERVE)	ENERGY 1863 kJ (445 cal)	PROTEIN 40.6 g	SODIUM 201 mg	FAT 16.3 g	SAT FAT 2.4 g	CARBOHYDRATE 29.7 g	SUGAR 12.5 g	FIBRE 8.2 g

CHORIZO, CHICKPEA AND GREEN OLIVE TAGINE

SERVES 4

Traditionally, a tagine is a large Moroccan pottery vessel with a flat circular base and a large cone-shaped top, which helps circulate steam in the dish, keeping the food moist. This recipe is a full-flavoured, quick-cooking tagine, and makes delicious leftovers.

1 tablespoon rice bran oil (or olive oil)

1 chorizo sausage, quartered lengthways and thinly sliced

1 red onion, halved and thinly sliced

200 g (7 oz/about ¼) butternut pumpkin (squash), peeled and cut into 1 cm (½ inch) cubes

3 garlic cloves, sliced

1 thumb-sized piece ginger, finely grated

2 tablespoons ground cumin

2 tablespoons ground coriander

375 ml (13 fl oz/1½ cups) salt-reduced chicken stock

6 fresh dates, pitted and sliced (available in the fruit and veg section of your supermarket)

2 handfuls kale leaves (or silverbeet/ Swiss chard), roughly chopped

400 g (14 oz) tinned chickpeas, rinsed and drained

60 g (2¼ oz/⅓ cup) Sicilian (green) olives, pitted and roughly chopped

2 tablespoons slivered almonds

130 g (4½ oz/⅔ cup) couscous

small handful flat-leaf (Italian) parsley, leaves picked, to serve

Heat a heavy-based frying pan (or a flameproof casserole dish or tagine dish) over medium–high heat. Add the rice bran oil, then the chorizo and cook for a minute or until fragrant. Add the onion and pumpkin. Cook, stirring occasionally, for 2–4 minutes or until the onion has softened. Add the garlic, ginger, cumin and ground coriander. Cook for 1–2 minutes until the garlic is translucent, then add the chicken stock, dates and kale. Increase the heat to high and cook, uncovered, for 3–5 minutes until the pumpkin is soft and the stock has reduced slightly. Stir through the chickpeas and olives, and scatter over the almonds. Remove from the heat.

Place the couscous in a bowl and pour over just enough boiling water to cover. Leave to sit for a minute, then fluff up the grains with a fork. Sprinkle over the parsley leaves then serve the tagine in the middle of the table with the couscous.

 NUTRITION TIP *Couscous, while delicious and convenient for this dish, is very refined—meaning it doesn't fill you up very quickly. Bulk out the couscous with nuts, herbs and even vegetables such as diced red onion or spring onion (scallions).*

SUBSTITUTION *Dates add a natural sweetness to this dish and help thicken the consistency by absorbing excess liquid. You could also use dried figs or currants. Wholemeal couscous is available at supermarkets and is a healthier choice.*

NUTRITION INFORMATION (PER SERVE)	ENERGY 1999 kJ (447 cal)	PROTEIN 15.8 g	SODIUM 144 mg	FAT 16.8 g	SAT FAT 2.7 g	CARBOHYDRATE 60.5 g	SUGAR 23.9 g	FIBRE 11.6 g

CRISPY SALMON WITH WINTER BRAISE

SERVES 4

Braising is an easy cooking technique that involves lightly pan-frying an ingredient, then continuing to cook it in a varying amount of liquid, to achieve maximum flavour. Served with the salmon, the braise in this dish make for a delicious and satisfying winter meal.

1 tablespoon rice bran oil (or olive oil), plus 1 tablespoon extra
1 leek, white part only, halved and thinly sliced lengthways
12 brussels sprouts, quartered
2 handfuls green beans, topped and tailed
3 garlic cloves, thinly sliced
8 thyme sprigs, leaves picked
60 ml (2 fl oz/¼ cup) salt-reduced chicken stock
4 x 180 g (6½ oz) salmon fillets, skin on
1 tablespoon olive oil
45 g (1½ oz/¼ cup) drained baby capers, rinsed
juice of 1 lemon

Heat 1 tablespoon of the rice bran oil in a large non-stick frying pan over high heat. Add the leek and brussels sprouts and cook, turning occasionally, for 3–5 minutes until golden brown and the leek has softened. Stir in the beans, garlic and thyme, then splash in the stock to help steam the beans. Cook for 2–3 minutes until the beans are slightly tender. Remove the vegetables from the pan and keep warm.

Wipe the pan out, then place back over high heat and add the remaining 1 tablespoon of rice bran oil. Add the salmon fillets to the pan, skin side down. Hold the fish down with an egg slide or spatula for the first 10 seconds to ensure the skin stays flat and gets nice and evenly crispy. Cook for 3–4 minutes, turn the fish over and cook for a further 2–3 minutes until cooked to your liking. Add the olive oil and capers to the pan for the final minute of cooking. Use a spoon to baste the oil and capers over the skin of the fish. Squeeze in the lemon juice and remove the pan from the heat.

Divide the braise among four plates and top with the salmon. Spoon some caper lemon sauce from the pan over the salmon and serve.

 NUTRITION TIP *Our body has the ability to produce most of the fats we require, except two: alpha-linolenic acid (omega-3 fatty acid) and linoleic acid (omega-6 fatty acid). Salmon is a rich source of both, and therefore a great inclusion in your diet.*

SUBSTITUTION *Try using other herbs to flavour your braise such as rosemary or oregano.*

NUTRITION INFORMATION (PER SERVE)	ENERGY 2308 kJ (551 cal)	PROTEIN 55.8 g	SODIUM 250 mg	FAT 32.5 g	SAT FAT 7.5 g	CARBOHYDRATE 6.1 g	SUGAR 4.3 g	FIBRE 6.7 g

PUMPKIN, BRUSSELS SPROUTS AND BLUE CHEESE PAPPARDELLE WITH PESTO

SERVES 4

This dish is not about the pasta. It's about the golden roasted vegetables and the bright green parsley pesto. The pasta is just there to carry the flavour. The roasted vegetables, salty and sour pesto and the rich creamy blue cheese all work deliciously together.

400 g (14 oz/about ½) butternut pumpkin (squash), peeled and cut into 1.5 cm (⅝ inch) pieces
2 handfuls brussels sprouts, halved
2 tablespoons olive oil
250 g (9 oz) dried pappardelle (or fettuccine)
1 handful flat-leaf (Italian) parsley, leaves picked
75 g (2½ oz) blue cheese, crumbled

PESTO
40 g (1½ oz/⅓ cup) walnuts
2 handfuls flat-leaf (Italian) parsley
1 small garlic clove
zest and juice of 1 lemon
2 tablespoons olive oil

Preheat the oven to 210°C (410°F/Gas 6–7).

Toss the pumpkin and brussels sprouts in the olive oil and season with a pinch of salt. Place on a baking tray and roast for 20–25 minutes until the vegetables are golden brown and tender. Add the walnuts (for the pesto) to the tray for the final 5 minutes, to toast.

To make the pesto, combine the toasted walnuts, parsley, garlic, lemon zest and juice in a small food processor and blitz to combine. Stir through the olive oil.

Cook the pappardelle according to the packet directions until *al dente*. Drain and stir through the parsley–walnut pesto. Divide among four bowls, top with the roasted pumpkin and brussels sprouts, crumble over the blue cheese, sprinkle over the parsley leaves and serve.

NUTRITION TIP *Unlike many pasta dishes, this recipe includes whole visible chunks of vegetables. The key when eating pasta is to make sure you fill the dish with vegetables and actually put effort into making these an enjoyable component of the dish.*

SUBSTITUTION *Gluten intolerant? Swap the pasta for quinoa and turn this dish into a warm salad.*

NUTRITION INFORMATION (PER SERVE)	ENERGY	PROTEIN	SODIUM	FAT	SAT FAT	CARBOHYDRATE	SUGAR	FIBRE
	2292 kJ (548 cal)	15.6 g	224 mg	28.1 g	6.8 g	53.7 g	7.7 g	8.1 g

SLOW-COOKED MOROCCAN LAMB WITH CAULIFLOWER 'COUSCOUS'

SERVES 6

While this dish is certainly not quick to cook, it *is* quick to prepare and convenient to serve. Do the preparation at the start of the day, leave it on a gentle heat, and when you return all the hard work is done.

600 g (1 lb 5 oz) piece lamb shoulder, cut into 3–4 cm (1¼–1½ inch) cubes
2 tablespoons plain (all-purpose) flour
2 tablespoons ground cumin
2 tablespoons ground coriander
1 tablespoon smoked paprika
2 tablespoons olive oil, plus 2 teaspoons extra
2 brown onions, sliced
400 g (14 oz) tinned chopped tomatoes
1 thumb-sized piece ginger, finely grated or chopped
2 cinnamon sticks (or 1½ teaspoons ground cinnamon)
500 ml (17 fl oz/2 cups) salt-reduced beef stock
600 g (1 lb 5 oz/½ head) cauliflower, broken into large chunks
75 g (2½ oz/½ cup) frozen peas
2 handfuls baby spinach
zest and juice of 1 orange
100 g (3½ oz) feta cheese, crumbled
3 handfuls flat-leaf (Italian) parsley, leaves picked

Preheat the oven to 120°C (235°F/Gas ½). Put the lamb pieces in a clean disposable plastic bag. Add the flour, cumin, coriander and paprika to the bag. Twist the bag closed and shake to cover the lamb in the spices and flour.

Heat a large flameproof heavy-based casserole dish over high heat. Add the olive oil, then add the lamb. Cook for 3–4 minutes until golden brown on all sides. Remove the lamb from the dish and set aside. Add the remaining 2 teaspoons of olive oil and the onion. Cook for 2–3 minutes or until the onion softens. Stir in the tomatoes, ginger, cinnamon and beef stock. Return the lamb to the dish. Transfer the pan to the oven, cover, and cook for 4 hours or until the lamb is tender. Carefully remove the dish from the oven. Set aside.

Place the cauliflower chunks in a food processor and blitz until it resembles couscous. Alternatively, grate the cauliflower on the large holes of a box grater. Heat 80 ml (2½ fl oz/⅓ cup) of water in a large frying pan over high heat. Add the cauliflower 'couscous' and peas, and stir for a minute. Cover, reduce the heat and cook for a further 3–4 minutes until tender. Remove from the heat and stir through the baby spinach and orange zest and juice.

Divide the cauliflower 'couscous' among four bowls. Top with the lamb mixture, feta and parsley, and serve.

NUTRITION TIP *Add firm root vegetables for the last cooking hour.*

SUBSTITUTION *Instead of lamb shoulder, use leg or pork shoulder.*

NUTRITION INFORMATION (PER SERVE)	ENERGY	PROTEIN	SODIUM	FAT	SAT FAT	CARBOHYDRATE	SUGAR	FIBRE
	1744 kJ (417 CAL)	29.8 g	678 mg	25.6 g	8.7 g	13.5 g	8.7 g	7.8 g

WINTER

FENNEL BRAISED MEATBALLS WITH POLENTA

Polenta has a subtle flavour, however, it absorbs flavour very well making it the perfect accompaniment to these meatballs and rich tomato sauce.

500 ml (17 fl oz/2 cups) salt-reduced chicken stock
95 g (3¼ oz/½ cup) instant polenta
20 g (¾ oz) parmesan cheese, grated
500 g (1 lb 2 oz) minced (ground) pork
2 tablespoons fennel seeds
1 tablespoon olive oil, plus
  1 tablespoon extra
1 long red chilli, thinly sliced
1 red capsicum (pepper), thinly sliced
½ fennel bulb, thinly sliced
4 garlic cloves, thinly sliced
700 ml (24 fl oz) tomato passata
  (puréed tomatoes)
2 handfuls rocket (arugula)
75 g (2½ oz/½ cup) pitted kalamata olives
1 pear, thinly sliced
1 tablespoon red wine vinegar

Line a 20 x 10 cm (8 x 4 inch) container with baking paper. Bring the chicken stock to the boil over high heat in a small saucepan. Whisk in the polenta until well combined. Reduce the heat to medium–low and cook for a further 2–3 minutes, stirring, until thickened. Remove from the heat and stir in the parmesan. Pour into the prepared container and refrigerate for 25–30 minutes or until set.

Meanwhile, put the pork mince in a bowl, add the fennel seeds and use your hands to combine well. Shape the pork mixture into 3 cm (1¼ inch) meatballs. Heat 1 tablespoon of the olive oil in a large, wide frying pan over high heat. Add the meatballs and cook, turning occasionally, for about 2 minutes until browned all over. Transfer the meatballs into a bowl and set aside.

In the same pan, add the chilli, capsicum, fennel and garlic. Cook over medium–high heat until the vegetables soften, then stir in the tomato passata. Bring to the boil, cook for 2–3 minutes, return the meatballs to the pan and reduce the heat to low. Cook for a further 3–5 minutes until the meatballs have just cooked through. Turn the polenta out onto a chopping board and cut into four pieces. Place the polenta pieces in a frying pan and cook over high heat for 1–2 minutes on each side until warmed through. Remove from the heat.

Toss the rocket, olives, pear, vinegar and remaining 1 tablespoon of oil together. Divide the polenta among four plates, top with the meatballs and serve with the rocket and pear salad.

NUTRITION TIP *Polenta is gluten-free.*

SUBSTITUTION *Try swapping the polenta for couscous.*

NUTRITION INFORMATION (PER SERVE)	ENERGY 2158 kJ (515 cal)	PROTEIN 33.7 g	SODIUM 1103 mg	FAT 28.4 g	SAT FAT 7.6 g	CARBOHYDRATE 27.8 g	SUGAR 12.2 g	FIBRE 8.5 g

CHOCOLATE BANANA MOUSSE, GRILLED BANANA AND PEANUTS

SERVES 4

Four ingredients and a seriously delicious dessert.
Chocolate, cream, banana and peanuts, it just works.

100 g (3½ oz/⅔ cup) chopped
   dark chocolate
2 tablespoons thickened (whipping)
   cream, plus 125 ml (4 fl oz/½ cup) extra
3 ripe small–medium bananas
35 g (1¼ oz/¼ cup) roasted peanuts

Combine the chocolate and 2 tablespoons of cream in a heatproof bowl and place over a small saucepan of simmering water. Make sure the base of the bowl does not touch the water so the chocolate doesn't burn or seize. Stir occasionally until melted and combined.

Meanwhile, put the remaining cream in a bowl. Use electric beaters or a whisk and whip to stiff peaks.

Remove the chocolate mixture from the heat, transfer to a small food processor and add one of the bananas. Blend until smooth. Fold the banana–chocolate mixture through the cream using a whisk.

Halve the remaining two bananas lengthways and grill (broil) or fry using a little spray oil in a hot pan for 1–2 minutes on each side until caramelised but not falling apart. Divide the caramelised bananas among four plates. Spoon the chocolate banana mousse over the top, add a scattering of peanuts and serve.

 NUTRITION TIP *For a healthier option and to make this dessert go further, add some orange and kiwi fruit to the grilled bananas.*

SUBSTITUTION *Swap the peanuts for roasted hazelnuts.*

NUTRITION INFORMATION (PER SERVE)	ENERGY 1566 kJ (374 cal)	PROTEIN 5.2 g	SODIUM 29 mg	FAT 26.7 g	SAT FAT 14.7 g	CARBOHYDRATE 28.9 g	SUGAR 24.0 g	FIBRE 2.4 g

GOAT'S CURD MOUSSE, WALNUT CRUMBLE AND ROASTED RHUBARB

SERVES 4

Rhubarb is usually stringy and bitter, but roasted rhubarb … well, let's just say it's not that! It's sweet, soft and tender, and together with the earthy walnut crumble complements the goat's curd perfectly.

4 rhubarb stalks, cut into
   4 cm (1½ inch) lengths
1 tablespoon honey, plus
   1 tablespoon extra
150 ml (5 fl oz) thickened
   (whipping) cream
1 teaspoon vanilla bean paste
   (or natural vanilla extract)
125 g (4½ oz) goat's curd
zest of 1 lemon
2 tablespoons plain (all-purpose) flour
1 tablespoon butter
1 tablespoon caster (superfine) sugar
¼ teaspoon ground cinnamon
30 g (1 oz) walnuts, crumbled into
   small pieces by hand

Preheat the oven to 200°C (400°F/Gas 6). Line a baking tray with baking paper.

Place the rhubarb onto the prepared tray and pour over the 1 tablespoon of honey. Mix briefly to combine. Transfer to the oven and cook for 10–15 minutes until tender but not completely falling apart. Check the rhubarb after 5 minutes—if it is starting to colour too much or burn, cover with a piece of foil. Remove from the oven, cover it lightly to keep warm and set aside.

Meanwhile, put the cream and vanilla bean paste in a bowl. Use electric beaters or a whisk and whip to stiff peaks. In a second bowl, use a spatula to beat together the goat's curd, lemon zest and remaining honey. Fold the cream mixture and goat's curd mixture together until well combined.

Rub together the flour, butter, sugar, cinnamon and walnuts in a small bowl. Tip the mixture into a dry frying pan and cook over medium–high heat for a few minutes, stirring, until golden and fragrant.

Spoon the goat's curd mousse into four serving glasses, top with the roasted rhubarb and the walnut crumble, and serve.

NUTRITION TIP *Replace the butter in the crumble with olive oil. This replaces saturated fats with healthy monounsaturated fats.*

SUBSTITUTION *Try roasted rhubarb with muesli and natural yoghurt for a delicious breakfast.*

NUTRITION INFORMATION (PER SERVE)	ENERGY	PROTEIN	SODIUM	FAT	SAT FAT	CARBOHYDRATE	SUGAR	FIBRE
	1435 kJ (343 cal)	10.4 g	164 mg	21.9 g	11.2 g	24.0 g	19.9 g	3.3 g

WINTER POACHED PEARS WITH WHIPPED RICOTTA

SERVES 6

Pears make a great poaching fruit due to their relatively firm consistency, which softens slightly once cooked. The pears absorb the flavours of the liquid and produce a visually stunning dessert. This dessert is refined and rich, but not too sweet.

500 ml (17 fl oz/2 cups) dry red wine

115 g (4 oz/⅓ cup) honey, plus 2 tablespoons extra

2 cinnamon sticks (or 1½ teaspoons ground cinnamon)

8 cloves

zest strips and juice of 1 orange

6 pears, peeled and cored, but leave the stem intact

125 ml (4 fl oz/½ cup) thickened (whipping) cream

250 g (9 oz) low-fat ricotta cheese (from a tub, not the deli section of your supermarket)

2 teaspoons vanilla bean paste (or natural vanilla extract)

50 g (1¾ oz/⅓ cup) chopped dark chocolate (70% cocoa)

1 tablespoon olive oil

25 g (1 oz/¼ cup) toasted flaked almonds

Combine the red wine, 115 g (4 oz/⅓ cup) of the honey, cinnamon, cloves, orange zest and juice in a saucepan. Add the pears and enough water to barely cover them. Bring to a gentle simmer over medium–high heat. Cover with a piece of baking paper and a small saucer or heatproof weight to help keep the pears below the surface of the liquid. Cook for 20–25 minutes until the pears can easily be pierced with a knife.

Meanwhile, put the cream in a bowl. Use electric beaters or a whisk and whip to stiff peaks, then whisk in the ricotta, vanilla bean paste and remaining honey. Set aside to serve.

Remove the cooked pears from the liquid and transfer to four serving bowls, then increase the heat to high and boil rapidly for 10–15 minutes until the liquid is reduced and thickened slightly.

Put the chocolate in a heatproof bowl and place over a small saucepan of simmering water. Make sure the base of the bowl does not touch the water, and stir occasionally until melted. Stir in the olive oil. Remove the cinnamon, cloves and zest from the pear liquid and discard. Spoon the syrup over the pears, top with the whipped ricotta and flaked almonds, drizzle with the chocolate sauce and serve.

 NUTRITION TIP *Dark chocolate adds a depth of flavour and the bitter richness reduces the likelihood of overconsumption.*

SUBSTITUTION *Try replacing the wine with water, and pop in a couple of chai-flavoured tea bags for extra flavour.*

WINTER

NUTRITION INFORMATION (PER SERVE)	ENERGY 1486 kJ (355 cal)	PROTEIN 7.3 g	SODIUM 113 mg	FAT 18.2 g	SAT FAT 8.6 g	CARBOHYDRATE 39.0 g	SUGAR 34.1 g	FIBRE 5.3 g

RHUBARB AND ORANGE FRANGIPANE

SERVES 8

This cake is fresh, zesty, sweet and sour. It's incredibly easy to prepare and makes an excellent lunchbox or office treat. Instead of only using butter, sugar and flour for our cake batter, we've included yoghurt and almond meal. This helps keep the cake moist and full flavoured.

olive oil spray, for greasing
2 oranges
60 g (2¼ oz/½ cup) icing (confectioners') sugar
3 tablespoons butter, softened
2 eggs
190 g (6¾ oz/⅔ cup) low-fat Greek–style yoghurt, plus 260 g (9¼ oz/1 cup) extra, to serve
135 g (4¾ oz/1⅓ cups) almond meal
35 g (1¼ oz/¼ cup) plain (all-purpose) flour
4 rhubarb stalks, cut into 3 cm (1¼ inch) pieces
honey, for brushing

Preheat the oven to 170°C (325°F/Gas 3). Grease a 20 cm (8 inch) springform cake tin and line the base and side with baking paper.

Zest the oranges into a large bowl. Peel the pith from the oranges and cut into segments then reserve these for serving. Add the icing sugar and butter to the zest and use electric beaters or a wooden spoon to beat for 1 minute or until the mixture is light and fluffy. Beat in 1 of the eggs and once it has been completely combined beat in the other egg. Stir through 190 g (6¾ oz/⅔ cup) of the yoghurt. Fold in the almond meal and flour until just combined.

Spoon the mixture into the prepared cake tin and flatten out a little with a spatula. Arrange the rhubarb pieces on top of the batter and press lightly into the surface. Bake for 25–30 minutes until an inserted skewer comes out clean. Remove from the oven, brush with honey and leave to cool in the tin.

Carefully remove the cake from the tin. Cut into wedges and serve with orange segments and the remaining yoghurt.

 NUTRITION TIP *Make this cake gluten-free by substituting the plain flour for gluten-free flour or more almond meal.*

SUBSTITUTION *If you want to prepare this dish in summer, use strawberries or blueberries instead of rhubarb.*

NUTRITION INFORMATION (PER SERVE)	ENERGY 1157 kJ (276 cal)	PROTEIN 10.5 g	SODIUM 73 mg	FAT 16.8 g	SAT FAT 5.0 g	CARBOHYDRATE 18.4 g	SUGAR 15.2 g	FIBRE 4.4 g

DARK CHOCOLATE, BEETROOT AND HAZELNUT BROWNIES

MAKES 16

Everybody loves a good brownie! These brownies are rich and moist, but we've managed to squeeze a couple of fruits and vegetables in, and some healthy fats, so you don't need to feel guilty when you enjoy a slice.

3 eggs
60 ml (2 fl oz/¼ cup) olive oil
60 g (2¼ oz/⅓ cup lightly packed)
   light brown sugar
200 g (7 oz/1⅓ cups) chopped dark
   chocolate
400 g (14 oz/about 2) small–medium
   beetroot (beets), peeled, cored
   and grated
1 pear, grated
135 g (4¾ oz/1⅓ cups) almond meal
55 g (2 oz/½ cup) Dutch cocoa,
   plus extra for dusting
55 g (2 oz) hazelnuts, chopped
1 teaspoon ground cinnamon

Preheat the oven to 160°C (315°F/Gas 2–3). Line a 20 cm (8 inch) square baking tin with baking paper.

Put the eggs, olive oil and sugar in a bowl and whisk together until the sugar has dissolved.

Put the chocolate in a heatproof bowl and place over a small saucepan of simmering water. Make sure the base of the bowl does not touch the water so the chocolate doesn't burn or seize. Stir occasionally until melted.

Whisk the melted chocolate into the egg mixture, then stir in the beetroot, pear, almond meal, cocoa, hazelnuts and cinnamon.

Transfer the batter to the prepared tin and bake for 25–30 minutes until the brownie is set and smells delicious. Leave the brownie to cool slightly before turning out and cutting into 5 cm (2 inch) square pieces. Dust with the extra cocoa and serve.

 NUTRITION TIP *This brownie is jam-packed with healthy ingredients, however, it is still high in energy, primarily from the healthy fats in the olive oil, almond meal and hazelnuts. Enjoy one small piece at a time.*

SUBSTITUTION *Try swapping the cinnamon for nutmeg or vanilla bean paste or even rosewater. These ingredients masquerade as 'sweet' spices and flavourings without the energy content of sugar.*

NUTRITION INFORMATION (PER PIECE)	ENERGY	PROTEIN	SODIUM	FAT	SAT FAT	CARBOHYDRATE	SUGAR	FIBRE
	909 kJ (217 cal)	4.9 g	35 mg	15.1 g	3.6 g	14.9 g	12.4 g	3.0 g

SPRING

FRESH. FLAVOURSOME. DELICATE.

After months of heavy rich comfort food we see relief in the form of peas, beans, asparagus and fennel. These spring greens are exactly what we want after we emerge from the cold of winter. Fruit orchards and vegetable patches burst into life and herbs such as mint, coriander and basil are back with a vengeance. We crave lighter satisfying meals such as Calamari with broad bean salad (page 180) and Spring lentil minestrone (page 189). Lighter soups also feature and chargrilled vegetables make a nice change from roasted. We even dabble in the return of refreshing, light and crispy salads, such as Coconut-poached chicken with Vietnamese salad (page 179). And, just to let us know that summer is approaching, strawberries really start to shine and begin to pave the way for other berries.

SPRING SHOPPING LIST

Spring is all about crisp, fresh, pencil-thin asparagus, soft but firm beans that burst with freshness and crispy sweet sugar snap peas. Asparagus is a rich source of vitamin K and a good source of vitamin A, folate and iron. Choose thin, firm asparagus and avoid woody or drooping spears. Store them in the fridge and cook them quickly to ensure they remain crisp and fresh, not stringy.

Spring fruits include strawberries, blood oranges, pineapple and rockmelon. These sweet yet slightly acidic fruits are bursting with nutrition and add colour and complexity to spring menus. Strawberries are an excellent source of vitamin C and manganese, which is important for bone formation and the metabolism of carbohydrate and protein.

VEGETABLES

- ASIAN GREENS
- ASPARAGUS
- BEAN SPROUTS
- BEETROOT (BEETS)
- BROAD (FAVA) BEANS
- BROCCOLI
- BRUSSELS SPROUTS
- CABBAGE
- CARROTS
- CAULIFLOWER
- CELERIAC
- CHILLIES
- CUCUMBER
- FENNEL
- GARLIC
- GLOBE ARTICHOKES
- GREEN BEANS
- GREEN ONIONS (SHALLOTS)
- LEEKS
- LETTUCE
- MUSHROOMS
- PEAS
- POTATOES
- SILVERBEET (SWISS CHARD)
- SPINACH
- SPRING ONIONS (SCALLIONS)
- SUGAR SNAP PEAS
- SWEETCORN
- TOMATOES
- WATERCRESS
- ZUCCHINI (COURGETTES)
- ZUCCHINI FLOWERS

FRUIT

- AVOCADOS
- BANANAS
- BLOOD ORANGES
- BLUEBERRIES
- CHERRIES
- GRAPEFRUIT
- HONEY MURCOTT MANDARINS
- LADY WILLIAMS APPLES
- LEMONS
- LOQUATS
- MANGOES
- MELONS
- MULBERRIES
- NAVEL ORANGES
- PAPAYA
- PASSIONFRUIT
- PINEAPPLES
- POMELO
- ROCKMELON
- SEVILLE ORANGES
- STRAWBERRIES
- TANGELOS
- VALENCIA ORANGES
- YOUNGBERRIES

PEA, MINT AND PROSCIUTTO BRUSCHETTA

SERVES 4

This dish is spring on a plate—colourful, light and fresh. The pea mixture is vibrant and zesty while the prosciutto is crispy and salty. It makes for a delicious brunch, light lunch or even a satisfying snack.

280 g (10 oz) freshly podded peas
(or defrosted frozen peas)
1 handful mint, leaves picked,
plus extra to serve
zest and juice of 2 lemons
3 prosciutto slices
4 thick slices dark rye bread
50 g (1¾ oz) feta cheese, crumbled

Blend together the peas, mint, lemon zest and juice in a food processor.

Heat a non-stick frying pan over medium–high heat. Add the prosciutto and cook for 1–2 minutes on each side until crisp. Remove to a chopping board, cool slightly, then roughly chop.

Toast the dark rye slices and divide among four plates, top each with a quarter of the pea mixture, the crumbled feta, prosciutto and extra mint leaves and serve.

 NUTRITION TIP *Choose heavy bread. The heavier the better! It's satisfying, high in fibre and full of nutrition including B vitamins, iron and more.*

SUBSTITUTION *Not a fan of prosciutto? Leave it off. Try thinly sliced fennel or even smoked salmon. Instead of feta try mozzarella or bocconcini.*

NUTRITION INFORMATION (PER SERVE)	ENERGY 926 kJ (221 cal)	PROTEIN 14.2 g	SODIUM 768 mg	FAT 6.5 g	SAT FAT 3.1 g	CARBOHYDRATE 22.4 g	SUGAR 3.5 g	FIBRE 8.3 g

INDIAN SCRAMBLED EGGS

SERVES 4

Deep, rich, spicy and creamy this recipe is our take on
a brekkie classic. Sunday brunch, here we come.

8 eggs
80 ml (2½ fl oz/⅓ cup) low-fat milk
1 tablespoon olive oil, plus
   1 tablespoon extra
200 g (7 oz) Swiss brown
   mushrooms, quartered
1 teaspoon cumin seeds
3 handfuls coriander (cilantro), leaves
   picked, stems finely chopped
1 teaspoon ground turmeric
cumin naan bread (see page 142—or
   store-bought), toasted, to serve
2 spring onions (scallions), thinly sliced
   on an angle (optional)

Crack the eggs into a bowl. Use a whisk or fork to beat the eggs
and milk together until just combined.

Heat a large, heavy-based frying pan or saucepan over high heat.
Add 1 tablespoon of the olive oil, the mushrooms, cumin seeds and
coriander stems to the pan. Cook for 3–4 minutes until the mushrooms
are golden brown and cooked through. Remove the mushrooms from
the pan and cover to keep warm. Reduce the heat to low. Add the
remaining oil to the pan, then stir in the turmeric and add the egg
mixture. Leave for 10–20 seconds before slowly folding the mixture
with a spatula or wooden spoon, making sure you get right to the
bottom and edge of the pan. Don't over-stir the eggs. When the eggs
are nearly cooked, remove from the heat—the eggs will continue to
cook after you take them from the stove.

Divide the naan among four serving plates, top with the scrambled
eggs, mushrooms, spring onion, if using, and reserved coriander leaves,
and serve.

 NUTRITION TIP *Eggs are a great source of quality protein
as well as antioxidants and omega-3 fats.*

SUBSTITUTION *Swap the naan bread for rye sourdough.
It will complement the eggs and will be very satisfying.*

NUTRITION INFORMATION (PER SERVE)	ENERGY	PROTEIN	SODIUM	FAT	SAT FAT	CARBOHYDRATE	SUGAR	FIBRE
	908 kJ (217 cal)	16.6 g	159 mg	14.5 g	4.0 g	4.3 g	3.0 g	2.3 g

HONEY SOY CHICKEN WITH GINGER NOODLES

SERVES 4

The whole family is sure to love this one. When cooking the mushrooms, be careful not to overcrowd the pan, and cook them in batches. This will help achieve that delicious golden colour.

2 tablespoons light soy sauce

1 tablespoon honey

2 tablespoons mirin

180 g (6½ oz) packet soba noodles

2 teaspoons sesame oil

1 tablespoon rice bran oil (or olive oil)

4 x 100 g (3½ oz) boneless, skinless chicken thighs, thinly sliced

2 tablespoons cornflour (cornstarch)

8 shiitake mushrooms, quartered (or Swiss brown or button mushrooms)

1 thumb-sized piece ginger, grated

6 bok choy (pak choy), quartered

2 handfuls baby spinach

2 tablespoons roasted, unsalted cashews, roughly chopped

Stir the soy sauce, honey and mirin together in a bowl until well combined. Set aside.

Bring a saucepan of water to a simmer and add the soba noodles. Cook according to the packet directions, then drain. Toss through the sesame oil and set aside.

Heat the rice bran oil in a large frying pan over high heat. Coat the sliced chicken in cornflour and add to the pan. Cook for 2–3 minutes on each side until browned, then add the honey soy sauce. Continue to cook, stirring, for a further minute or until the chicken is just cooked through and the sauce sticks. Remove from the pan and set aside.

Add the mushrooms and ginger to the same pan and cook, stirring, for 30 seconds to allow the mushrooms to soak up any leftover sauce. Add the bok choy, spinach and 125 ml (4 fl oz/½ cup) of water to help the vegetables steam. Cook for 1–2 minutes until the water evaporates, then stir through the sesame noodles.

Divide the vegetables among four serving plates, top with the chicken and cashews, and serve.

NUTRITION TIP *Soba noodles are traditionally made from buckwheat, however, commercially available ones are made using a mixture of grains, so check the label if your are gluten intolerant.*

SUBSTITUTION *Any leafy green will substitute easily for the bok choy in this recipe.*

NUTRITION INFORMATION (PER SERVE)	ENERGY 1949 kJ (466 cal)	PROTEIN 22.8 g	SODIUM 544 mg	FAT 28.7 g	SAT FAT 7.1 g	CARBOHYDRATE 27.2 g	SUGAR 9.5 g	FIBRE 5.7 g

SMOKED SALMON AND ASPARAGUS NIÇOISE SALAD

SERVES 4

Traditional, French 'salade Niçoise', consists of tomatoes, tuna, hard-boiled eggs, anchovies and olives, along with potato. Our version includes green beans, asparagus and beautiful hot smoked salmon. This is not a light and leafy side, it's a bulky, satisfying complete meal.

4 eggs
8 new potatoes, quartered
2 handfuls green beans, topped and tailed
8 asparagus spears, woody ends snapped off, halved
juice of 2 lemons
1 tablespoon dijon mustard
60 ml (2 fl oz/¼ cup) olive oil
250 g (9 oz) hot smoked salmon, flaked
2 baby cos (romaine) lettuce, leaves separated
55 g (2 oz/⅓ cup) pitted kalamata olives
2 handfuls dill, leaves picked

Place the eggs in a large saucepan and cover with cold water. Bring to the boil over high heat, then reduce the heat to low and very gently simmer for 10 minutes. Drain the eggs and cover in cold water to stop the cooking process. Peel the eggs and discard the shells. Leave them to cool slightly, then cut lengthways into quarters.

Bring a saucepan of water to the boil. Add the potatoes and boil for 10–15 minutes or until tender. Drain well, then transfer the potatoes into a large bowl and set aside.

Add more water to the saucepan and bring to the boil then add the beans and asparagus. Cook for 2–3 minutes or until bright green and slightly tender. Drain and immerse in a large bowl of cold water to stop the cooking process. Drain well. Add to the potatoes.

Whisk together the lemon juice, mustard and olive oil in a small bowl.

Add the eggs, salmon, lettuce, olives and dill to the salad. Gently toss through the lemon dressing. Divide among four plates and serve.

 NUTRITION TIP *This salad is fresh, healthy and balanced. Consider exchanging the potato for low-GI sweet potato.*

SUBSTITUTION *Swap the smoked salmon for another protein, such as grilled fish or chicken.*

NUTRITION INFORMATION (PER SERVE)	ENERGY	PROTEIN	SODIUM	FAT	SAT FAT	CARBOHYDRATE	SUGAR	FIBRE
	1951 kJ (466 cal)	29.2 g	1174 mg	24.4 g	4.7 g	27.3 g	4.8 g	9.0 g

COCONUT-POACHED CHICKEN WITH VIETNAMESE SALAD

SERVES 4

There's a tendency for people to overcook chicken breast, which makes it dry and stringy. Poaching is a great way to overcome this—the chicken breast gently cooks while it is immersed in liquid, which helps to ensure it remains moist and tender.

1½ tablespoons fish sauce
1 tablespoon light brown sugar
juice of 2 limes (or 1 lemon)
1 long red chilli, seeded and thinly sliced
2 carrots, finely grated or julienned
2 handfuls snow peas (mangetout), trimmed and thinly sliced lengthways
115 g (4 oz/1 cup) bean sprouts
2 handfuls mint, leaves picked
2 granny smith apples, finely grated or julienned
35 g (1¼ oz/¼ cup) roasted peanuts

COCONUT-POACHED CHICKEN
400 ml (14 fl oz) tinned low-fat coconut milk
500 ml (17 fl oz/2 cups) salt-reduced chicken stock (or water)
1 thumb-sized piece ginger, thinly sliced on an angle
3 handfuls coriander (cilantro), roots and stems roughly chopped, leaves reserved
2 x 250 g (9 oz) boneless, skinless chicken breasts

To make the coconut-poached chicken, combine the coconut milk, chicken stock, ginger and coriander roots and stems in a saucepan. Bring to the boil over high heat, then reduce the heat to a simmer and add the chicken. If the chicken isn't submerged, add just enough water to cover. Simmer very gently (very! Just the odd bubble should emerge) for 15 minutes or until the chicken is just cooked. Remove the saucepan from the heat and leave the chicken to sit in the liquid for a further 5 minutes before removing. Set aside until cool enough to handle, then shred the chicken meat.

Meanwhile, strain the coconut broth and reserve as a base for soup, curry or more poached chicken on another day.

Stir the fish sauce, sugar, lime juice and chilli together in a bowl until the sugar has dissolved.

Combine the carrot, snow peas, bean sprouts, mint leaves, half the coriander leaves and the apple in a large bowl. Mix through the shredded chicken, pour over the dressing and gently combine. Divide among four serving plates, top with the peanuts and remaining coriander leaves, then serve.

 NUTRITION TIP *Poaching is a very healthy cooking technique—it does not require any oil, flour, crumbs, butter or eggs.*

SUBSTITUTION *Reduce the fat content of this recipe by poaching the chicken in stock or water only.*

NUTRITION INFORMATION (PER SERVE)	ENERGY 1250 kJ (299 cal)	PROTEIN 34.1 g	SODIUM 921 mg	FAT 8.4 g	SAT FAT 2.9 g	CARBOHYDRATE 18.6 g	SUGAR 16.3 g	FIBRE 6.5 g

CALAMARI WITH BROAD BEAN SALAD

SERVES 4

Calamari is so much more than salt and pepper squid! It is lean, affordable and cooks super quickly. Prepare all the other elements of your meal first and then cook the calamari at the very last minute.

BROAD BEAN SALAD

2 oranges
2 tablespoons white wine vinegar
2 tablespoons capers, rinsed, plus
   2 tablespoons extra
3 handfuls flat-leaf (Italian) parsley,
   leaves picked
2 teaspoons dijon mustard
1 tablespoon olive oil
185 g (6½ oz/1 cup) podded broad (fava)
   beans (or podded frozen broad beans)
2 French shallots, thinly sliced
3 radishes, thinly sliced
400 g (14 oz) tinned cannellini beans,
   rinsed and drained

4 calamari tubes
2 tablespoons rice bran oil (or olive oil)

Finely grate the zest of 1 orange into a small food processor. Add the white wine vinegar, capers, parsley and mustard and blitz until smooth, then stir through the olive oil.

Half-fill a small saucepan with hot water and bring to the boil. Add the broad beans, cook for 2–3 minutes until just tender but still bright green. Drain, rinse thoroughly with cold water and drain again. Cut both oranges into segments and place into a large salad bowl. Add the broad beans, shallot, radish and cannellini beans to the salad bowl. Set aside.

Use a sharp knife to slice the calamari tubes open. Score the calamari on a 45-degree angle at 5 mm (¼ inch) intervals—be careful not to slice all the way through the calamari. Turn the calamari 90 degrees and score again. Cut the scored calamari into 5 x 3 cm (2 x 1¼ inch) rectangles.

Heat the rice bran oil in a large frying pan over high heat. Add the calamari pieces in batches and cook for 30 seconds, tossing around, or until the calamari turns white and curls up.

Combine the caper–parsley dressing and the salad, and divide among four plates. Top with the calamari and extra capers, and serve.

 NUTRITION TIP *Broad beans provide a good source of low-GI carbohydrate and protein, fibre and folate.*

SUBSTITUTION *This salad works well with almost any seafood.*

NUTRITION INFORMATION (PER SERVE)	ENERGY 999 kJ (239 cal)	PROTEIN 18.4 g	SODIUM 330 mg	FAT 10.5 g	SAT FAT 1.8 g	CARBOHYDRATE 12.6 g	SUGAR 6.0 g	FIBRE 9.1 g

LEMONGRASS AND GINGER POACHED SALMON WITH BOK CHOY AND EGG NOODLES

SERVES 4

This dish is full of flavour, bright in colour and nutritionally balanced, which for a broth- or soup-based dish is a big positive. It makes the most of new-season spring greens, and is a perfect meal as we transition from the cooler winter days into the spring sunshine.

400 ml (14 fl oz) low-fat coconut milk
1 tablespoon fish sauce
1 tablespoon light brown sugar
2 lemongrass stems, bruised
1 thumb-sized piece ginger, finely grated
3 kaffir lime leaves, torn (or leaves from a lemon tree)
4 x 150 g (5½ oz) skinless salmon fillets
3 bok choy (pak choy), quartered
3 celery stalks, sliced into 1 cm (½ inch) diagonal strips
2 handfuls snow peas (mangetout), trimmed
200 g (7 oz) egg noodles, boiled until just tender, to serve
1 long red chilli, seeded and thinly sliced
1 handful basil or Thai basil, leaves picked
1 lemon, cut into cheeks, to serve

Combine the coconut milk, fish sauce, sugar, lemongrass, ginger, lime leaves and 125 ml (4 fl oz/½ cup) of water in a large saucepan. Bring to a gentle simmer over medium heat and cook for 5–10 minutes for the flavours to infuse.

Add the fish to the saucepan and cook for 3 minutes, then add the bok choy, celery and snow peas. Cook for a further 2–3 minutes until the fish flakes apart when tested with tongs.

Divide the egg noodles among four serving bowls. Carefully divide the fish and greens among the bowls, ladle the broth over and top with the chilli and basil leaves. Serve with lemon cheeks to squeeze over.

 NUTRITION TIP *Low-fat coconut milk is thinner in texture and contains about half the fat compared to full fat. It is essentially diluted coconut cream, which provides a happy middle ground in terms of flavour and fat.*

SUBSTITUTION *If egg noodles aren't your thing, serve this dish with brown rice. It will soak up the flavoursome sauce and thicken the dish.*

NUTRITION INFORMATION (PER SERVE)	ENERGY 2313 kJ (552 cal)	PROTEIN 51.3 g	SODIUM 677 mg	FAT 27.0 g	SAT FAT 11.6 g	CARBOHYDRATE 22.8 g	SUGAR 6.8 g	FIBRE 7.2 g

MUSSELS, TOMATO AND FENNEL LINGUINE

Mussels are perceived as being difficult to cook when in fact they couldn't be easier. They offer such great flavour, are affordable and work deliciously well in soups, curries and pastas.

2 tablespoons olive oil

½ fennel bulb, thinly sliced

3 handfuls basil, stems finely chopped, leaves picked and reserved

4 spring onions (scallions), thinly sliced

3 garlic cloves, thinly sliced

1 tablespoon fennel seeds

2 teaspoons smoked paprika

700 ml (24 fl oz) tomato passata (puréed tomatoes)

250 g (9 oz) linguine (or another long pasta)

1 kg (2 lb 4 oz) mussels, cleaned and debearded

2 zucchini (courgettes), shaved into strips using a vegetable peeler

Heat the olive oil in a large saucepan over high heat. Add the fennel, basil stems, spring onion, garlic and fennel seeds. Cook for 2–3 minutes until the fennel softens slightly. Stir in the paprika and passata. Simmer for 10 minutes or until the sauce darkens slightly in colour.

Bring a second large saucepan of water to the boil and add the linguine. Cook according to the packet directions or until *al dente*.

When the pasta is almost cooked, add the mussels to the tomato sauce and cover with a lid.

Drain the cooked pasta and toss through the mussels and tomato sauce along with the shaved zucchini. Divide among four bowls, top with the basil leaves and serve.

 NUTRITION TIP *Mussels are an excellent source of vitamin B12, which is important for the production of normal red blood cells, and brain and nervous system functionality.*

SUBSTITUTION *Consider using other types of seafood in this recipe, including prawns (shrimp), scallops, crab or maybe even all of them!*

NUTRITION INFORMATION (PER SERVE)	ENERGY 1880 kJ (449 cal)	PROTEIN 22.0 g	SODIUM 503 mg	FAT 13.2 g	SAT FAT 2.4 g	CARBOHYDRATE 56.5 g	SUGAR 8.9 g	FIBRE 8.2 g

SPICED LAMB WITH ASPARAGUS, BROCCOLINI AND BROWN RICE

SERVES 4

Brown rice has a lovely nutty flavour and texture. These characteristics match the whole spices in this recipe very well, with pan-fried asparagus, broccolini and roasted almonds all contributing to a crunchy dish that is very satisfying.

50 g (1¾ oz/¼ cup) brown rice
1 teaspoon cumin seeds
1 teaspoon fennel seeds
400 g (14 oz) lamb backstrap (or lamb loin chops or cutlets)
1 tablespoon rice bran oil (or olive oil)
12 asparagus spears, woody ends snapped off
200 g (7 oz/1 bunch) broccolini
5 thyme sprigs
2 tablespoons roasted almonds, roughly chopped
2 tablespoons currants
1 handful flat-leaf (Italian) parsley, finely chopped
juice of ½ lemon
1 tablespoon olive oil

Put the brown rice in a saucepan with plenty of water. Bring to the boil over high heat and then cook for 18–22 minutes until tender. Drain well and set aside.

Toast the cumin seeds and fennel seeds in a hot dry frying pan over medium–high heat for 1 minute or until fragrant. Grind the spices in a food processor or use a mortar and pestle. Rub the spice mixture over the lamb.

Heat the rice bran oil in a non-stick frying pan over high heat. Add the lamb and cook for 3–4 minutes on each side until golden brown and cooked to your liking. Remove the lamb from the pan and leave to rest, lightly covered.

Add the asparagus, broccolini and thyme to the pan and cook for 2–3 minutes until tender.

Combine the brown rice, almonds, currants, parsley, lemon juice and olive oil in a bowl. Divide among four plates and top with the asparagus and broccolini. Thinly slice the lamb and place on top of the vegetables and serve.

 NUTRITION TIP *Half a cup of cooked brown rice is a serve. Limit your portions rather than completely eliminating rice.*

SUBSTITUTION *Thyme adds great flavour, but you could also use rosemary, sage or any hard stem herb or spices, such as chilli flakes.*

NUTRITION INFORMATION (PER SERVE)	ENERGY	PROTEIN	SODIUM	FAT	SAT FAT	CARBOHYDRATE	SUGAR	FIBRE
	1442 kJ (344 cal)	24.9 g	80 mg	19.5 g	4.8 g	15.4 g	5.3 g	4.8 g

MUSHROOM AND BROCCOLINI PAD THAI

SERVES 4

Pad Thai should be light and fresh, unlike most versions of the popular takeaway which are usually stodgy and sweet. Our pad Thai is balanced and full of vegetables, colours and textures.

3 tablespoons tamarind paste
1 tablespoon light brown sugar
2 tablespoons light soy sauce
80 g (2¾ oz) flat rice noodles
400 g (14 oz/2 bunches) broccolini
1 teaspoon rice bran oil (or olive oil),
    plus 2 tablespoons extra
250 g (9 oz) mushrooms, sliced
    (try to get different varieties)
2 French shallots, thinly sliced
2 eggs
100 g (3½ oz) firm tofu, diced
2 tablespoons peanuts, chopped
3 handfuls coriander (cilantro), leaves
    picked, stems finely chopped
85 g (3 oz/⅔ cup) bean sprouts
3 spring onions (scallions), thinly
    sliced on an angle
1 lime or lemon, cut into cheeks, to serve

Mix the tamarind paste, sugar and soy sauce together in a small bowl.

Cook the noodles in a saucepan of boiling water for 2–4 minutes until just tender. Add the broccolini for the last minute of cooking. Drain and toss in the 1 teaspoon of rice bran oil to keep the noodles from sticking together.

Heat the remaining oil in a large non-stick frying pan or wok over high heat. Add the mushrooms and fry for 2–3 minutes until browned, then remove from the pan and set aside. Add the shallot to the pan and cook for 1–2 minutes until lightly golden, then crack in the eggs and mix it around with a wooden spoon for 1–2 minutes until the egg is almost cooked. Add the diced tofu, peanuts and coriander stems and stir for 30 seconds or until fragrant. Return the mushrooms to the pan, add the noodles, broccolini and the tamarind dressing, then move the noodles around with tongs until the liquid has been absorbed. Add half the bean sprouts and spring onion, mix in quickly, then remove from the heat.

Divide the pad Thai among four bowls and serve with the remaining beans sprouts and spring onion, lime or lemon cheeks and the coriander leaves.

NUTRITION TIP *Use gluten-free soy sauce or fish sauce to make this dish coeliac friendly.*

SUBSTITUTION *Thai and Chinese cuisines substitute ingredients very well. In fact, at many restaurants you are often given a choice of protein. Try adding some prawns (shrimp) or shredded chicken.*

NUTRITION INFORMATION (PER SERVE)	ENERGY	PROTEIN	SODIUM	FAT	SAT FAT	CARBOHYDRATE	SUGAR	FIBRE
	1276 kJ (305 cal)	17.4 g	956 mg	18.3 g	3.1 g	14.2 g	8.9 g	8.5 g

SPRING LENTIL MINESTRONE

SERVES 6

As you can see from our recipes we believe in lots of vegetables and food that requires you to really chew and think about what you are eating. A variety of textures makes a meal interesting and also satisfying. This soup is no exception.

2 tablespoons olive oil

2 bacon rashers, thinly sliced

3 spring onions (scallions), thinly sliced

1 carrot, diced

1 celery stalk, diced

3 garlic cloves, sliced

2 teaspoons caraway seeds

60 g (2¼ oz) lentils

1.5 litres (52 fl oz/6 cups) salt-reduced chicken stock

200 g (7 oz/1 head) broccoli, chopped into florets

1 zucchini (courgette), diced

6 asparagus spears, woody ends snapped off, cut into 3 cm (1¼ inch) lengths

1 handful tarragon (or flat-leaf/Italian parsley), leaves picked

6 slices crusty bread, to serve

Heat the olive oil in a large saucepan over medium heat. Add the bacon, spring onion, carrot, and celery and leave to cook for a minute, then give it a stir with a wooden spoon. Add the garlic. Continue to stir occasionally for 3–4 minutes until the ingredients turn golden brown. Add the caraway seeds and lentils, stir, then pour in the stock. Simmer for 25 minutes or until the lentils are tender.

Add the broccoli, zucchini and asparagus to the pan and cook for 3–5 minutes until the vegetables are tender but still bright green. Ladle the minestrone into six serving bowls, top with the tarragon and serve with crusty bread.

NUTRITION TIP *Don't fall into the trap of filling up on bread when eating soup. Enjoy a small amount, but get stuck into the soup where all the flavour is!*

SUBSTITUTION *Instead of the lentils try chickpeas, white beans, pearl barley or freekeh.*

NUTRITION INFORMATION (PER SERVE)	ENERGY 1048 kJ (250 cal)	PROTEIN 12.7 g	SODIUM 1413 mg	FAT 10.3 g	SAT FAT 2.1 g	CARBOHYDRATE 24.8 g	SUGAR 3.3 g	FIBRE 5.2 g

BAKED ZUCCHINI IN BOLOGNESE SAUCE

SERVES 6

Now just so you know, we don't have any problems with pasta, in fact we love it! However, making lasagne can be a little time consuming, so this dish is designed to help people produce a similar baked dish in less time and with the inclusion of a very noticeable extra vegetable.

1 tablespoon olive oil
1 brown onion, finely chopped
1 large carrot, finely chopped
1 celery stalk, finely chopped
3 garlic cloves, sliced
3 handfuls basil, leaves reserved,
  stems finely chopped
2 teaspoons fennel seeds
2 teaspoons allspice
500 g (1 lb 2 oz) minced (ground) beef
400 g (14 oz) tinned chopped tomatoes
700 ml (24 fl oz) tomato passata
  (puréed tomatoes)
6 zucchinis (courgettes)
75 g (2½ oz/½ cup) pitted
  kalamata olives
80 g (2¾ oz) feta cheese, crumbled,
  to serve
wholegrain crusty bread, to serve

Preheat the oven to 190°C (375°F/Gas 5).

Heat the olive oil in a heavy-based saucepan over high heat. Add the onion, carrot and celery and cook for 3–5 minutes until softened. Stir in the garlic, basil stems, fennel seeds and allspice, then add the beef and cook for 5–10 minutes, stirring occasionally, until evenly browned. Stir in the tomatoes and passata. Reduce the heat and simmer the bolognese gently while you prepare the zucchini.

Halve the zucchini lengthways. Lay the 8 zucchini halves cut side facing up in a snug-fitting baking dish. Carefully pour the bolognese over the top to cover the zucchini completely, top with the olives, then bake for 40–45 minutes until the zucchini is tender when pierced with a knife.

Top the baked zucchini with the feta and basil leaves. Serve in the middle of the table with wholegrain crusty bread.

NUTRITION TIP *Just because there's no pasta in this dish, it doesn't mean you can eat twice the amount. There is still plenty of energy in the sauce.*

SUBSTITUTION *Try swapping the zucchini for small eggplants (aubergines). Give the eggplants a drizzle of olive oil and a head start in the oven, and once they have softened top with the bolognese sauce.*

NUTRITION INFORMATION (PER SERVE)	ENERGY	PROTEIN	SODIUM	FAT	SAT FAT	CARBOHYDRATE	SUGAR	FIBRE
	1770 kJ (423 cal)	32.0 g	686 mg	19.2 g	7.0 g	26.6 g	10.7 g	7.0 g

LAMB WITH CHARRED SPRING ONIONS, PEA PURÉE AND SWEET POTATO WEDGES

SERVES 4

Lamb and peas, two spring greats. 'Spring lamb' refers to the seasonal peak in supply due to the breeding cycle. The flavour of spring lamb is usually sweet as the lambs graze on fresh spring grass.

2 sweet potatoes, cut into thin wedges
1 tablespoon olive oil, plus
    1 tablespoon extra
1 garlic clove, crushed
80 ml (2½ fl oz/⅓ cup) low-fat
    pouring (whipping) cream
215 g (7½ oz/1½ cups) frozen peas,
    defrosted
125 ml (4 fl oz/½ cup) salt-reduced
    chicken stock (or water)
small handful mint, leaves picked
zest and juice of a lemon
8 lamb loin chops or cutlets
    (about 50 g/1¾ oz each)
10 spring onions, halved lengthways

Preheat the oven to 220°C (425°F/Gas 7). Line a baking tray with baking paper.

Combine the sweet potato wedges and 1 tablespoon of the olive oil in a bowl and toss to combine. Transfer onto the prepared tray and roast for 30–40 minutes until the wedges are tender when pierced with a knife.

When the wedges are almost cooked, combine the garlic and cream in a saucepan and bring to a simmer over medium heat. Add the peas and chicken stock and cook for a minute to warm the peas through. Add the mint, lemon zest and juice, then remove from the heat and purée with a stick blender until smooth. Set aside.

Heat the remaining oil in a frying pan over high heat. Add the lamb and cook for 2–3 minutes on each side or until golden brown and cooked to your liking. Remove from the pan and set aside, lightly covered, to rest.

Add the spring onions to the pan and cook for 2–3 minutes or until softened and lightly charred. Serve the lamb with the pea purée, spring onions and sweet potato wedges.

 NUTRITION TIP *Sweet potato offers a lower glycaemic option compared to other white potatoes, however, it still contains energy so portion control is important.*

SUBSTITUTION *We think pea purée is absolutely delicious, however, if you disagree try a cauliflower purée.*

NUTRITION INFORMATION (PER SERVE)	ENERGY	PROTEIN	SODIUM	FAT	SAT FAT	CARBOHYDRATE	SUGAR	FIBRE
	1557 kJ (372 cal)	34.5 g	219 mg	15.9 g	5.9 g	20.0 g	9.3 g	6.7 g

FENNEL-CRUSTED PORK WITH GREEN APPLE SLAW

SERVES 4

This recipe will have dinner on the table in under twenty minutes. The fennel seeds add flavour to the pork quickly and they also provide a crunchy crust. The slaw is light and fresh and the granny smith apple adds a sweet acidity, which balances the fennel-crusted pork.

1½ tablespoons fennel seeds
4 x 150 g (5½ oz) pork loin steaks
1 tablespoon rice bran oil (or olive oil)
130 g (4½ oz/½ cup) low-fat
    Greek-style yoghurt
2 tablespoons wholegrain mustard
1 small handful flat-leaf (Italian)
    parsley leaves, torn

GREEN APPLE SLAW
2 granny smith apples, julienned
    or finely grated
3 radishes, thinly sliced
½ small fennel bulb, thinly sliced
200 g (7 oz/about ⅛) purple cabbage,
    thinly sliced
1 small handful flat-leaf (Italian)
    parsley leaves, torn
30 g (1 oz/¼ cup) walnuts, very
    roughly chopped
2 tablespoons lemon juice
2 tablespoons olive oil

Toast the fennel seeds in a hot non-stick frying pan over high heat for 1 minute or until fragrant. Tip into a small food processor, or use a mortar and pestle, and blitz until coarsely ground. Rub the ground fennel seeds over the pork.

Using the same pan, heat the rice bran oil over high heat. Add the pork and cook for 3–4 minutes on each side until a deep golden brown. Remove from the pan and leave to rest, lightly covered, for a few minutes.

Meanwhile, combine the apple, radish, fennel, purple cabbage, parsley and walnuts in a bowl. Pour over the lemon juice and olive oil, and stir to combine. Taste and adjust the balance of flavours with a little more lemon juice or olive oil if needed.

Stir together the yoghurt and mustard. Divide the slaw among four serving plates. Slice the pork and place on top of the slaw, top with the parsley, spoon over the mustard yoghurt and serve.

 NUTRITION TIP *Pork loin is low in fat, very high in thiamin and a complete source of quality protein.*

SUBSTITUTION *This slaw makes the perfect shared salad for a spring barbecue or a delicious sandwich filling.*

SPRING

NUTRITION INFORMATION (PER SERVE)	ENERGY	PROTEIN	SODIUM	FAT	SAT FAT	CARBOHYDRATE	SUGAR	FIBRE
	1727 kJ (413 cal)	39.3 g	306 mg	20.1 g	3.2 g	16.1 g	14.0 g	6.1 g

ASPARAGUS, DILL AND FISH RISOTTO

SERVES 4

Most people think you need to slave over the stove to make risotto. Take the hassle and time out of the process by adding generous amounts of liquid, stirring the mixture briefly to combine. Then leave it to cook until the liquid has nearly evaporated before repeating this step.

1 litre (35 fl oz/4 cups) salt-reduced chicken stock
1 tablespoon olive oil
1 brown onion, finely diced
5 thyme sprigs, leaves picked
3 garlic cloves, sliced
220 g (7¾ oz/1 cups) arborio rice
1 lemon
2 teaspoons rice bran oil (or olive oil)
4 x 120 g (4¼ oz) fish fillets such as salmon or barramundi, skin on
about 16 asparagus spears, woody ends snapped off, sliced into 3 cm (1 inch) lengths, tips left whole
200 g (7 oz/1 head) broccoli, chopped into florets
75 g (2½ oz/½ cup) frozen peas
1 small handful dill, roughly chopped
60 g (2¼ oz) feta cheese, crumbled

Bring the stock to the boil in a saucepan over high heat, then remove from the heat, set aside and keep warm.

Heat the olive oil in a saucepan over medium heat. Add the onion, thyme and garlic and cook, stirring, until translucent. Add the rice and stir for 30 seconds to toast it. Zest the lemon and add to the pan along with the juice. Add a ladleful of the stock and simmer. Add more stock as required throughout the process to make sure the rice is just covered with liquid. Stir occasionally. The risotto will take about 16–18 minutes to cook. If you run out of stock before this time, use a little hot water.

Meanwhile, heat the rice bran oil in a large frying pan over high heat. Add the fish and cook for 2–3 minutes on each side until a skewer can easily be inserted, or until just starting to flake apart. Remove the fish from the pan and set aside, lightly covered. Add the asparagus and broccoli to the pan and cook, stirring, for 2 minutes or until the vegetables are bright green and almost tender. Add the peas and stir for a minute to defrost them. Remove from the heat.

When the rice is *al dente*, stir in the vegetables and dill. Divide among four bowls, top with the fish and feta, and serve.

NUTRITION TIP *Risotto is high in carbohydrate. Make sure to bulk it out with vegetables and protein like this recipe does.*

SUBSTITUTION *Once you know how to make the rice base you can make any risotto you choose. Mushroom risotto, duck risotto …*

NUTRITION INFORMATION (PER SERVE)	ENERGY	PROTEIN	SODIUM	FAT	SAT FAT	CARBOHYDRATE	SUGAR	FIBRE
	1966 kJ (470 cal)	37.5 g	1293 mg	11.5 g	3.1 g	49.5 g	3.4 g	7.4 g

INSTANT BANANA ICE CREAM WITH SESAME PRALINE

SERVES 4

This is the perfect use for those leftover dark bananas. It's quick, easy and once you try it you will have a constant supply of bananas in the freezer.

3 tablespoons caster (superfine) sugar
2 tablespoons sesame seeds (white, black or a combination all work)
3 bananas, peeled, thinly sliced and frozen in a snap lock bag or container
2 tablespoons Frangelico (hazelnut liqueur)

To make the praline, line a baking tray with baking paper. Put the sugar in a small saucepan, add 2 tablespoons of water and heat gently over low heat until the sugar has dissolved, then increase the heat and cook until it turns amber in colour. Add the sesame seeds, give it a stir, then pour onto the lined tray. Leave to cool before breaking up into smaller pieces.

To make the instant banana ice cream, combine the frozen banana and Frangelico in a food processor and blend until smooth and creamy. If there are any lumps, scrape the mixture down with a spatula and blend briefly again.

Serve the ice cream in dessert glasses topped with the praline.

 NUTRITION TIP *Because bananas have a naturally creamy texture this ice cream does not rely on a traditional creamy custard base, making this dessert a much healthier alternative.*

SUBSTITUTION *Swap the Frangelico for coffee for a delicious banana coffee ice cream, or make this dish kid friendly by using low-fat cream. Sesame allergy? Try chia seeds or chopped pepitas (pumpkin seeds) instead.*

NUTRITION INFORMATION (PER SERVE)	ENERGY 774 kJ (185 cal)	PROTEIN 2.9 g	SODIUM 11 mg	FAT 5.4 g	SAT FAT 1.5 g	CARBOHYDRATE 28.8 g	SUGAR 26.5 g	FIBRE 2.4 g

BARBECUED PINEAPPLE WITH MINT SYRUP

SERVES 4

This dessert is light and refreshing, and super simple. You can make the syrup in advance so that all you need to do is grill the pineapple and then add the toppings.

90 g (3¼ oz/¼ cup) honey
2 handfuls mint, leaves picked
juice of 1 lime
½ pineapple, skin and core removed,
   cut into 8 thin wedges lengthways
4 scoops vanilla bean ice cream, to serve
30 g (1 oz/¼ cup) toasted macadamia
   nuts, roughly chopped

Combine the honey, half the mint leaves, the lime juice and 60 ml (2 fl oz/¼ cup) of water in a small saucepan over medium high heat. Simmer gently for 2–3 minutes until a light syrup forms. Remove from the heat. Discard the mint leaves.

Preheat a barbecue (or chargrill or frying pan) to high heat. Add the pineapple wedges and cook for 2–3 minutes each side or until lightly charred. For the last minute of cooking, use a pastry brush to baste the pineapple with a little of the mint syrup.

Divide the pineapple among four serving plates, top each plate with a scoop of ice cream, the remaining mint syrup, the macadamias and the remaining mint leaves, and serve.

 NUTRITION TIP *Macadamia nuts are higher in fat and lower in protein than most nuts, hence their rich creamy texture. Enjoy these in small amounts in dishes rather than simply snacking on them individually.*

SUBSTITUTION *If you are out of mint, try making a ginger and lemon zest syrup or a lavender syrup—or perhaps even a lavender and tarragon syrup.*

NUTRITION INFORMATION (PER SERVE)	ENERGY 908 kJ (217 cal)	PROTEIN 2.6 g	SODIUM 22 mg	FAT 8.7 g	SAT FAT 2.7 g	CARBOHYDRATE 31.3 g	SUGAR 30.1 g	FIBRE 3.0 g

ROASTED STRAWBERRY AND RHUBARB FOOL

SERVES 4

Strawberries are often the first berry to hit the shelves in spring, before the summer berries follow around four to eight weeks later. Roasted strawberries may have you feeling a little confused, but the soft texture and intensified sweetness are delicious.

4 rhubarb stalks, cut into 3–4 cm (1¼–1½ inch) pieces
500 g (1 lb 2 oz) strawberries, hulled and halved
1 tablespoon honey, plus 1 tablespoon extra
250 ml (9 fl oz/1 cup) thickened (whipping) cream
1 teaspoon vanilla bean paste (or natural vanilla extract)
40 g (1½ oz/¼ cup) pepitas (pumpkin seeds)

Preheat the oven to 200°C (400°F/Gas 6). Line a baking tray with baking paper.

Place the rhubarb and half the strawberries on the prepared tray and pour over 1 tablespoon of honey. Mix briefly to combine. Transfer to the oven and cook for 10–15 minutes until tender but not completely falling apart. Check the rhubarb and strawberries after 5 minutes—if they are starting to colour or burn too much, cover them with a piece of foil. Remove from the oven and leave to cool.

Whip the cream, remaining honey and the vanilla to stiff peaks. Fold through the roasted rhubarb and strawberries along with any syrup from the baking tray. Add the remaining fresh strawberries. Spoon into four glasses and serve topped with the pepitas.

NUTRITION TIP *Strawberries are a good source of fibre and vitamin C and are low in sugar.*

SUBSTITUTION *As the summer fruits begin to appear, swap the rhubarb for peaches or apricots.*

NUTRITION INFORMATION (PER SERVE)	ENERGY	PROTEIN	SODIUM	FAT	SAT FAT	CARBOHYDRATE	SUGAR	FIBRE
	1575 kJ (376 cal)	7.7 g	48 mg	28.1 g	15.9 g	20.5 g	19.2 g	4.6 g

DESPITE THEIR SWEET TASTE,
STRAWBERRIES ARE NOT HIGH IN SUGAR.
IN FACT, 10 JELLY BEANS HAVE THE SAME AMOUNT OF SUGAR AS 55 STRAWBERRIES!

LEMON, CHIA AND CHAI FRIANDS

MAKES 8

A friand is a small French cake made using almond meal, egg whites, butter and sugar. We have flavoured our friands using lemons, honey and chai tea. These friands are super moist and zesty. They are also gluten free, and therefore perfect for people with coeliac disease.

2 lemons
3 chai tea bags
90 g (3¼ oz/¼ cup) honey
1 thumb-sized piece ginger, sliced thinly
80 g (2¾ oz) butter
110 g (3¾ oz/½ cup) caster (superfine) sugar
3 eggs
200 g (7 oz/¾ cup) low-fat Greek-style yoghurt, plus extra to serve
150 g (5½ oz 1½ cups) almond meal
3 tablespoons chia seeds

Preheat the oven to 160°C (315°F/Gas 2–3). Grease and line 8 holes of a 12-hole friand or muffin tray.

Finely grate the zest of both lemons into a large mixing bowl (reserve a little in a small bowl for serving) and set aside. Juice both lemons into a small saucepan and add the chai tea bags, honey and ginger. Bring to the boil over high heat and cook for 5 minutes or until it smells delicious and has thickened slightly. Discard the tea bags and ginger.

Add the butter and sugar to the lemon zest bowl. Beat together using electric beaters or a wooden spoon until light and creamy. Beat in the eggs, one at a time, then beat in the yoghurt until just combined. Fold through the almond meal and chia seeds. Stir through the chai syrup. Divide the mixture among 8 holes of the friand or muffin tray. Bake for 20–25 minutes until an inserted skewer comes out with only a few crumbs clinging to it. Remove from the oven. Set aside until cool enough to handle.

Remove the friands from the pan. Serve with a dollop of yoghurt and a sprinkle of the reserved lemon zest.

 NUTRITION TIP *This is a great gluten-free treat. It has those desirable moist characteristics that most gluten-free desserts usually lack.*

SUBSTITUTION *Try including a little thyme or rosemary to add a delicious savoury tone to the friands.*

NUTRITION INFORMATION (PER FRIAND)	ENERGY	PROTEIN	SODIUM	FAT	SAT FAT	CARBOHYDRATE	SUGAR	FIBRE
	1418 kJ (339 cal)	9.0 g	111 mg	22.5 g	6.7 g	24.5 g	24.5 g	3.5 g

KIWI FRUIT AND MINT SORBET WITH CHOCOLATE CRUMBLE

SERVES 4

This instant sorbet takes only minutes to assemble. Have your kiwi fruit peeled, diced and frozen and your crumble made in advance and stored in an airtight container for times when you need a healthy instant dessert.

4 kiwi fruit
2 tablespoons light brown sugar
2 tablespoons rice bran oil (or olive oil)
35 g (1¼ oz/⅓ cup) almond meal
30 g (1 oz/¼ cup) Dutch cocoa
½ teaspoon ground cinnamon
1 large handful mint, leaves picked
125 ml (4 fl oz/½ cup) apple juice

Use a sharp knife to remove the skin from the kiwi fruit. Cut each kiwi fruit into slices and transfer to a snap-lock bag or airtight container. Freeze for 2–4 hours or overnight.

Put the sugar, rice bran oil, almond meal, cocoa and cinnamon in a bowl and rub together, using your fingertips, until combined.

Heat a non-stick frying pan over high heat. Add the crumble mixture and cook, stirring, for 2–3 minutes until fragrant. Tip back into the bowl and leave to cool.

Put the mint leaves in a small food processor (reserve a little in a small bowl for serving). Add the frozen kiwi fruit and apple juice and blend until smooth. Divide the kiwi fruit and mint sorbet among four bowls, top with the chocolate crumble and extra mint, and serve.

 NUTRITION TIP *Try swapping the butter for olive oil in the crumble. This will reduce the saturated fat and increase the healthy fat content. Just add the oil slowly and be careful not to make the mixture too wet.*

SUBSTITUTION *Swap the kiwi fruit for frozen raspberries or mango. These will accompany the chocolate crumble perfectly.*

NUTRITION INFORMATION (PER SERVE)	ENERGY	PROTEIN	SODIUM	FAT	SAT FAT	CARBOHYDRATE	SUGAR	FIBRE
	998 kJ (238 cal)	4.4 g	28 mg	15.2 g	2.5 g	18.3 g	16.4 g	6.4 g

VANILLA BAKED RICOTTA WITH STRAWBERRIES AND BALSAMIC SYRUP

SERVES 4

Ricotta is a super versatile ingredient. It carries flavour well and can therefore be used in sweet and savoury dishes. The sweet and slightly acidic balsamic strawberries will balance the rich ricotta nicely.

olive oil spray, for greasing
caster (superfine) sugar, for dusting
250 g (9 oz) low-fat ricotta cheese
   (from a tub, not the deli section
   of your supermarket)
2 eggs
1 teaspoon vanilla bean paste
   (or natural vanilla extract)
1 tablespoon rosewater (optional)
30 g (1 oz/¼ cup) icing (confectioners')
   sugar, sifted
125 ml (4 fl oz/½ cup) balsamic vinegar
2 tablespoons honey
250 g (9 oz) strawberries,
   quartered lengthways
2 tablespoons pistachio nuts, chopped

Preheat the oven to 200°C (400°/Gas 6). Grease the inside of four ramekins with spray oil, then dust the insides with caster sugar. Shake out any excess.

Combine the ricotta, eggs, vanilla bean paste, rosewater, if using, and icing sugar in a large bowl. Divide the mixture among the ramekins, then transfer to the oven and bake for 15–25 minutes until golden brown and relatively firm in the middle. Remove from the oven and leave to cool for at least 15 minutes.

Meanwhile, combine the balsamic vinegar and honey in a small saucepan. Boil over high heat for 3–5 minutes until the bubbles slow down slightly to form a light syrup. Pour into a small bowl and leave to cool and thicken.

Once the ramekins are cool enough to handle, carefully turn the baked ricotta upside down onto plates and serve with the strawberries, balsamic syrup and chopped pistachios.

 NUTRITION TIP *If rosewater does not appeal to you, try replacing it with a little squeeze of lime or elderflower cordial. However, because cordial is sweeter you will need to reduce the icing sugar by approximately half.*

SUBSTITUTION *Serve the baked ricotta with the roasted strawberries from page 200 instead of these fresh strawberries with balsamic syrup.*

NUTRITION INFORMATION (PER SERVE)	ENERGY 948 kJ (226 cal)	PROTEIN 12.8 g	SODIUM 17 mg	FAT 8.5 g	SAT FAT 2.4 g	CARBOHYDRATE	SUGAR 23.0 g	FIBRE 1.3 g

INDEX

ACKNOWLEDGEMENTS

This book would not have been possible without the guidance, advice, assistance and support of many people.

To Murdoch Books. Thank you for meeting with Callum and me and for seeing the value in our book and food philosophy, and for believing in us. We thoroughly enjoyed working with you.

To our amazing staff at Sprout. Thank you for working longer, covering our shifts and for being generally understanding during some stressful times! None of this would be possible without you.

To my family and friends, this book is for you. A sign of what love, belief and support can help you achieve.

To Callum, this is one serious milestone, but I know this is only one of many more that we will achieve at Sprout.

To my wife, Sam, thanks for being patient, thanks for listening to me during times of crazy book writing and work stress, thanks for always being there and thanks for sitting next to me, proofreading and helping me during those sleepless nights. Thanks also for letting me work on the book during our honeymoon ...

To you, the readers, I hope you love *Quick.Easy.Healthy.*

Themis

Thanks to my dad who made me fall in love with food.

Thanks to the wonderful Murdoch Books for helping me write my third book and my first book with Themis! I feel incredibly lucky to work with such a great team.

To the Sprout team, you are the best people I could ever hope to work with and you have all in some way contributed to us being able to write this book.

To Kirsty, Mum and Greg, thanks for your constant help, support and love.

To Themis, whatever happened to our one cooking class a month? It's great to work alongside someone so passionate, knowledgeable and driven. Looking forward to our next adventure!

To Crystal, Kane, Kyle, Josh and all my friends, thanks for being so understanding, and for sharing a beer in stressful times!

To the most important people, YOU, the readers, as without you there are no books. I hope this book inspires you to eat, laugh and have fun in the kitchen.

Callum

Published in 2016 by Murdoch Books, an imprint of Allen & Unwin.

For Corporate Orders & Custom Publishing contact Noel Hammond,
National Business Development Manager, Murdoch Books Australia

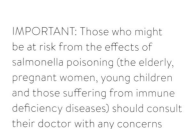
Murdoch Books Australia
83 Alexander Street
Crows Nest NSW 2065
Phone: +61 (0) 2 8425 0100
Fax: +61 (0) 2 9906 2218
www.murdochbooks.com.au
info@murdochbooks.com.au

Murdoch Books UK
Erico House, 6th Floor
93–99 Upper Richmond Road
Putney, London SW15 2TG
Phone: +44 (0) 20 8785 5995
Fax: +44 (0) 20 8785 5985
www.murdochbooks.co.uk
info@murdochbooks.co.uk

Publisher: Diana Hill
Design Manager: Hugh Ford
Designer: Madeleine Kane
Editor: Emma Hutchinson
Photographer: Alan Benson
Stylist: Rhianne Contreras
Home Economist: Grace Campbell
Production Manager: Alexandra Gonzalez

Text copyright © Callum Hann and Themis Chryssidis 2016
Design copyright © Murdoch Books 2016
Photography copyright © Alan Benson 2016

A cataloguing-in-publication entry is available from the catalogue
of the National Library of Australia at www.nla.gov.au.
A catalogue record for this book is available from the British Library.

Colour reproduction by Splitting Image, Clayton, Victoria.
Printed by Hang Tai Printing Company Limited, China.

IMPORTANT: Those who might
be at risk from the effects of
salmonella poisoning (the elderly,
pregnant women, young children
and those suffering from immune
deficiency diseases) should consult
their doctor with any concerns
about eating raw eggs.

OVEN GUIDE:
You may find cooking times vary
depending on the oven you are using.
For fan-forced ovens, as a general
rule, set the oven temperature to
20°C (35°F) lower than indicated
in the recipe.

MEASURES GUIDE: We have used
20 ml (4 teaspoon) tablespoon
measures. If you are using a 15 ml
(3 teaspoon) tablespoon add an
extra teaspoon of the ingredient
for each tablespoon specified.